Solway Sunrise

The Shooting Times and Country Magazine—November 15, 1952

INQUEST ON PARTRIDGES
by J. Wentworth Day

The
SHOOTING TIMES
and Country Magazine

SEVENTIETH YEAR   SATURDAY, NOVEMBER 15th, 1952   1s/3d WEEKLY

The Shooting Times and Country Magazine—November 15, 1952

THE DAWN SHOT

1840   **1952**

T. BLAND & SONS (Gunmakers) LTD.

NEW GUNS

Hammerless 12 Bores from £57 . 10 . 0 to £225 . 10 . 0.
3″ 12 Bore Brent Guns, £63 . 0 . 0, inc. Tax.
  (Send for Illustrated Folder.)
New Single Barrel 12 Bore Guns, B.S.A., £18 . 2 . 11. Webley, £17 . 18 . 4.
New Single barrel, Bolt action Webley 410 Guns. £9 . 7 . 6.

PUNT GUNS

Blands New 1½″ Screw Breech Gun, £125 . 0 . 0.

GUN REPAIRS

To all makes of Guns, New Barrels, Restocking, Overhauls, Recolouring, etc. Estimates
  Free. Prices Strictly Moderate.

CARTRIDGES

4, 8, 10, 12, 16, 20, 28 & 410 Bores : Alphamax, Maximum, Grand Prix, Bland Felt-
  wad, etc. (Price List on Application.)

RIFLES

22 B.S.A. Sportsman " 5," £8 . 5 . 0 ; " 15," £9 . 10 . 0 ; Brno, Winchester and
  Beretta Rifles, etc.

ACCESSORIES

		EVERYTHING FOR THE SHOOTER
Mallard Duck Decoys ...	£2 . 2 . 0 pair	
Wigeon Decoys... ...	£2 . 9 . 0 pair	Game Carriers and Bags, Cartridge Bags and Belts, Gun Cases and Covers, Cleaning Rods, etc. (Let us know your requirements and we will do our best to supply.)
Teal Decoys	£2 . 9 . 0 pair	
Wooden Feeding Pigeons	£1 . 2 . 6 each	
Improved Pigeon Decoys	4 . 6 each	Sole Agents for " English Guns and Rifles," by J. N. George, 37/6. (Trade enquiries invited.)
Silent Dog Whistles ...	15 . 4 each	

4 & 8 WILLIAM IV STREET, WEST STRAND, W.C.2

(TEMple Bar 9122)

This book is number **325** *of a limited edition of 600 copies.*

Solway Sunrise

The Complete 'Ferryman' Stories
Edited and Compiled by
Desmond Batley

The 'Ferryman' articles are reproduced with courtesy of the family of Willie Hughes / *The Shooting Times and Country Magazine.*

G C Books would like to thank Michael Clayton for the care and attention to detail in the design and layout of both book and jacket.

Photographs

All photographs are reproduced with courtesy of the Hughes family, with the exception of the portrait of Adam Birrell (Creetown Museum & Peter Howie, Creetown) and the *Creetown Annie* (John Scoular). Jacket and page background images © 2008 Michael Clayton. Other images courtesy of *The Shooting Times & Country Magazine.*

ISBN 9781872350196

Published by:
G C Books Ltd,
Unit 10 Bladnoch Bridge Estate,
Bladnoch,
Wigtown.
DG8 9AB
email: gcbooks@btinternet.com
www.gcbooks.co.uk

Printed and bound by Cromwell Press, Trowbridge, Wiltshire.

Contents

Willie Hughes

Introduction

The idea for this book came about as often happens by accident. While on a visit to the Creetown Heritage Museum, I saw a mock up of a Gunning Punt fitted with a de-activated gun. Upon enquiry, I found that it had been the property of Willie Hughes, who wrote articles for the Shooting Times & Country Magazine during the late 1960s and early 1970s.

Having read some of the articles and being intrigued by them at the time, I decided to find out more about Wildfowling in the Creetown area of the Solway Firth and also if possible more about Willie himself.

Andrew Macdonald, Chairman of the Museum, kindly loaned me a small tape that Willie had made many years ago and also provided me with a list of names to follow up. This led to a series of meetings with people scattered as far apart as Aberdeen and the Isle of Whithom. Creetown Wildfowlers Chairman, Jim Petrie, invited me to attend one of their monthly meetings and there I met Hugh Grey, who features in some of Willie's stories and is still an active wildfowler. They also arranged for me to meet Howard Hughes, Willie's son who was to provide me with all his fathers papers relating to his wildfowling experiences over many years.

My Father, by Howard Hughes

Willie Gowan Hughes 1904 to 1989, was born and bred in Creetown, the Ferrytown O'Cree as it was previously known because of the ferry service which took travellers across the estuary of the river Cree from the Stewartry of Kirkcudbright into the Shire of Wigtown. The male population of the town were known as Ferrymen and it is no surprise that my father took this as his *nom de plume* when, in the fifties, he began to write wildfowling stories for the Shooting Times and Country Magazine. What gave him an interest in the sport is a little more difficult to understand for his father Bob Hughes had absolutely no interest in shooting but was totally absorbed in his love of music. Bob successfully led the Creetown Prize Silver Band for most of his life and my father played the euphonium and his brother Jack the trombone for many years. One of my earliest boyhood memories was of the band parading up St Johns Street in Creetown with dad and uncle Jack tootling away with gusto in the ranks while at the front but on the pavement and not on the road was Granda Hughes all five foot six inches of him, resplendent in his double breasted bandmasters uniform cutting a swath through the ranks of the onlooking townsfolk who reverently stepped back to 'let the bandmaster through'. Apparently that was the way it was done, with bags of style!

Times were hard in those days, a granite settmaker as Bob Hughes was earning maybe four or five pounds a week and boys were encouraged to find a bit of useful employment to supplement the family income. This caused Willie to gravitate towards the Fishhouse where the local salmon fishers the Birrells operated. Situated on a little promontory overlooking the Cree estuary and the bay the Fishhouse had an almost magical and mysterious feel about it which I experienced years later. It seemed to represent the history of the village particularly that holy of holys, the back room, which was banned to boys but was frequented by wise old pipe smoking men, where the fire was ignited by tarry rope and tea was served with condensed milk. In there, what tales were recounted. Heroic encounters, expeditions, exploits, war stories, prodigious tales of hunting, shooting and fishing. That candle lit room heard them all and if as a boy you were allowed in to bring sticks for the fire or some other chore then you would linger as long as you could to try to hear what the men were discussing, before the inevitable "get oot o' here boy" echoed in your ear and you were forced to scuttle for the door before a size ten Hood Bullseye connected with your rear.

It was here that my fathers interest in wildfowling and punting took root. The Birrells; Adam and his brother Willie supplemented their winter income by, amongst other things, wildfowling and punt gunning and very accomplished puntsmen they were too. They also had by nature of their work a detailed knowledge of the estuary and the bay. Apart from salmon fishing they fished for shrimps, sparling and white fish, way down the bay right to the 'green water' and this gave them invaluable knowledge of the terrain. Noting young Willie Hughes' zeal for fowling, Adam allowed him to use his black punt nicknamed the 'Coffin' to cross the Cree to Barsalloch Merse and the Bishop Burn where in winter many thousands of wigeon and greylag geese could often be found grazing on the short sweet grass. A wildfowler's paradise. Over the years my father was first invited to share punting expeditions with Adam and then when he was considered to be sufficiently competent he was allowed to borrow the Coffin and use the small punt gun, something of the order of a ten bore, which was mounted on the front. For much of my fathers life food rationing was the norm. It should be remembered that rationing began as far back as January 1918 and carried on in one shape or another until July 1954 when amongst other things the rationing of butcher's meat ended. There was therefore during these long years not only pressure from families for the men to do a fair bit of hunter-gathering but also there was a ready market in the cities for any game or fowl which could be used to supplement the meagre rations. Throughout the 1940s and 1950s bags of ducks and geese were sent by rail from Creetown Station to Alex Freeland & Son, Wholesale Salmon Merchants, Fish, Game, Rabbit & Poultry Salesmen; Fishmarket, Glasgow C.1. With geese fetching as high as 18 shillings and 6 pence; mallard 5 shillings; wigeon up to 3 shillings and 9 pence, and teal 2 shillings, cheques for as much as £3/5/9d, less commission were received throughout the season and were very welcome. The odd 'piner' goose was occasionally slipped into the bag but the hawkeyed salesmen were usually up to it and the sales slip would be returned with a comment such as 'l Greylag (thin) 5/-'. On rare occasions an unofficially obtained pheasant or partridge would find its way into the bag. To avoid embarassment to any of those involved , who might or might not have the appropriate Game Licence these were identified but the code name of SRs and JSRs (Scandinivian Rabbits were pheasants and Junior Scandinavian Rabbits were partridges). How my father used to chuckle at the thought of having fooled the authorities with the SR / JSR code. Ducks were also sold to regular customers round the village as well as being given to family members to supplement their diets.

The Hughes' also had a coop opposite the Old Quay. This was low net which was set in the winter months to catch flounders, dabs and codling. Long lines baited with lug worm, which had to be laboriously dug down near Carsluith, were also set off the Scaur opposite Milligans Granite Works. The cod lines were hard work but could be very productive with regular catches of twenty to thirty codling and dabs. Consignments of fish were regularly sent to Glasgow and were also sold to Plunkets the fishmongers in nearby Newton Stewart. These 'local' deliveries were often made by bicycle , a journey of some fourteen miles return. They were also made by bus and I well remember as a wee boy being put on the bus at Creetown with a big dripping bag of codling to take to Mr Plunket. I got off the bus at Dashwood Square no doubt to the relief of the other passengers and made my way to Plunkets entering the premises by the van entrance at the side. Archie Plunket was in the shop and was explaining to a rather posh looking lady customer that he was very sorry but due to transport problems, he had no fish. Out of the comer of his eye he saw me lurking in the doorway with my dripping bag of codling and without pausing for breath he carried on about Plunkets reputation for never letting the customer down before announcing that he had just received word, presumably from on high, that a 'fresh consignment has just come in'. Filleting knife in hand he then bore down upon me and proceeded to remove and expertly slice two choice cod for the lady. Another satisfied customer Archie!

All these activities kept my father very much in touch with his and indeed all our roots, the countryside and Mother Nature. He was an out and out country man and understood well that a crop could be taken from nature without it upsetting the balance. In this regard he loved nothing more that a night out long-netting rabbits, a day ferreting or decoying pigeons. At the same time he studied books on birds and on the flora and fauna of the country and was recognised as an authority particularly on the bird life of the area. Locals would regularly call at the house for advice on birds with broken wings, young fallen from nests and so on and all enquiries were sympathetically dealt with. Many creatures were nursed back to health before being released back into the wild. Not least of these was Rab the Raven which was discovered at nearby Ravenshall with a badly damaged wing. Rab became my friend during his convalesence and would sit on a special hessian perch on the front handlebars of my bike leaning into the wind as we sped round Creetown.As he got fitter so the complaints from neighbours began to roll in. Rab would sit on nearby roofs and watch the good womenfolk hang out their washing, he would then swoop down and systematically pull out all the pegs allowing sheets and smalls to fall to the muddy ground. He also had a fascination for bare ankles and would sneak up behind unsuspecting locals and deliver a deft peck to the unprotected area before flapping away with a chuckly croak. I have to confess that I had a tear in my eye when my father took me aside and advised that the time was overdue for Rab to be returned to the wild. We took him in a cardboard box tied to the front of my bike where he usually sat and we peddled off up to Gatehouse Station which was within sight of the Glints of Drumore which was the haunt of ravens and let Rab fly away. The hope was that he would meet up with some of his fellows and be happy. My wish was that he would make his way back to our home. He never did.

In addition to his detailed knowledge of the estuary, fathers job in the quarry also gave him an extra edge when it came to punting. Pounding away all day at the granite with a hand held hammer and a stone chisel or a twist drill gave him an incredibly strong and muscular right arm. He was almost in the 'Popeye' class. This meant that he could propel a punt against currents and at speed when other mere mortals struggled.His strength was often crucial in the latter stages of a set when, with the birds getting a bit anxious, he could close to effective range better than anyone. He grew up of course with some of the best puntsmen of the time Adam and Willie Birrell , Major Hulse and Christopher Dalgety. He also rubbed shoulders with some famous figures who visited Creetown and particularly the Fish House for seasonal punting forays. These included the late Sir Peter Scott and the famous actor of the day James Robertson Justice. There was a code of conduct when visiting puntsmen came to Creetown, that it would be mutually agreed by discussion who would go down the bay, who would go upriver and so on. That way everyone got a fair chance of a shot. In the event of any disagreement Adam Birrell had the final say.

My fathers punting apprenticeship could not have been in better hands. The Birrells and Major Hulse were acknowledged as being in the premier division of puntsmen and that they were willing to share a berth, so to speak, with him showed to all that he had arrived as a puntsman. This gave him the necessary credibility with visiting fowlers who were only too happy to let him show them the bay and the rivers. On all these many trips he never took payment, being content to freely share his knowledge with fellow punting enthusiasts. Sadly no records exist of these early years for although both my father and his brother Jack, who accompanied him on many an expedition did keep a game book and record details of bags etc., these were lost during a 'spring clean' by Grannie, (Gaga). Willie punted from 1917 when he was aged thirteen but it was not until 1939 that he acquired his own punt and punt gun bought from a retiring puntsman in Wigtown. This episode is wonderfully recorded in his article 'The Punt' which was first published in *The Shooting Times and Country Magazine* on 6th June 1970.

With his own outfit which included 'Gus', the name given to the muzzle loading punt gun which fired nineteen ounces of BB shot, he enjoyed many, many forays from his favourite anchorage at Slittery Point in the Ferry Burn near Creetown. His brother Jack most often accompanied him as did one of the Dalgettys or Gus Cockerel or one of the Luptons.

Eventually on 24th November 1956 I was considered competent enough to accompany my father on my first punting expedition. The Game book record reads as follows: *'Went out in punt with Dad, fine frosty morning, lots of mallard in the Ferry Burnout, could not see them in the moonlight. Tried a shot with 12 bore but missed. Had shot with punt gun (my first) in the Gut, at about ten ducks which we thought might be mallard. When smoke cleared, found I had got six which proved to be wigeon, quite happy with that. Reloaded and went down to Bladnoch. Had second shot there. Picked up eight wigeon and two shovellers. Lost one or two others swept down into choppy water. Dad shot two more wigeon on Barholm on the way home. Bag: 16 wigeon, 2 shoveller. Total 18.'* What the Game book did not say but what I remember vividly to this day was: 'when without the necessary go ahead, I fired at the mallard with the 12 bore and missed. "What the b...y blazes are you shooting at. That shot could scare every b...y duck out of the parish. Put that gun down and help me bale this punt".' And unrecorded details of that first shot: *'out of Ferry Burn, me right down, Dad half down quietly poleing, turn right into the Gut, glassy calm, 40 yards wide, pushing up 80 yards, blobs on side, dabbling in the shallow water: Ducks! ten or a dozen, just enough for a shot, closer and closer, line up, take lanyard, head to the side, Pull! smoke, relief, got some!'*

That was the start for me and over the years to come what great times we had out punting and shore shooting in all weathers. Seeing nature close up and learning, learning, learning about the wonders we had right on our own doorstep and of course meeting kindred spirits and making never-to-be-forgotten friendships It is on this subject that I would like to conclude this introduction to the wildfowling life of my father Willie Hughes. I must start with the Birrells; Adam and his brother Willie who took him under their wing and taught and guided him not only in the art of wildfowling and punting but also in the standards expected from those who participated in the sport. He took these aboard at the time and carried them through his entire career. I must mention G.T. Wilkins (Pat Wilkins) who was like a brother to my father. A keen wildfowler and nature photographer, Pat lived in Norfolk but had a house at Burnfoot near Carsluith and used to bring up shooting friends to enjoy the sport on the Solway. It was he who persuaded my father that his old double punt had seen better days and that the bulge midway up the barrel of Gus the old muzzle loader, was a sign that he was getting a bit tired and needed replacing. Between them they had built a fine new double punt, constructed to the dimensions recommended by that doyen of puntsmen Ralph Payne Galway and it was Pat who secured a new breech loading Thomas Bland Punt gun. My father did reluctantly accept that the new gun was safer and was easier to operate but it was 'No half the killer o' Gus'.

This leads on nicely to the last of my fathers special punting friends, Gus Cockrell. Gus enjoyed writing poetry and in 1949 sent my father seasonal greetings accompanied by a poem he had written entitled 'Punt Gunning'.

Punt Gunning

You wake up and listen for gale or for rain
You look at the clock then turn in again
For it's still a bit early even to start
All the things to be done in the cold and the dark
Like starting the car and hitching the trailer
Checking the gear, even down to the baler.

But at last it is time and you creep out of bed,
Your wife mutters something 'bout waking the dead
Sea boots, duffle clothes, wool and the rest
And you find yourself wishing for a fur undervest.

Then a drive along roads of water and ice
That crackle like glass that is caught in a vice
Then on to the marsh to the creeks which seems miles
Unloading the punt with its snags and its trials.

With the punt and its gun ready up on the bank
You back the car out of the hole where it sank
You then have to launch through the mud and the slime
For you're working the last of the ebb at the time.

So the water's well out and the mud banks are steep
You go off like a dog sledge when the huskey dogs leap
But you stick to the bottom in mud just like glue
You toil and you sweat 'till you're almost wet through.

But at last you're afloat and the mud's all washed off
For your punt must be white like the wings of a moth
By this time of course your feet are wet through
For your boots are made by the Attlee crew.

Now out on the flats, wings rustle and roar
Like a waterfall heard on the wind in a thaw
For they're washing and diving and shaking their tails
In the fresh that is running now after the gales
Whistling and purring, they're all of a charm
You can hear them for miles before dawn in a calm.

As you glide past the mudbanks on the last of the tide
Avoiding stray curlew perched up on the side
To say nothing of redshank, that horrible pest
As excuse for a noise they endlessly quest.

Then a single goose flies, close by overhead
How you are tempted to meet it with lead
But if you should use your little 12 bore
It could put all the wigeon away with a roar.

And the chance of a lifetime you might have got
If it hadn't been for taking this tempting shot
You set your teeth and let it go
and glide on into the eastern glow.

It will soon be too clear if you don't get on faster
The first light on your punt could cause a disaster
There's a thousand and one things can go astray
Without you getting the light the wrong way.

There are eddies and shallows and small bits of rock
Or the curse of the puntsman the noisy scull lock
Or a shot from a shore gun will often be heard
As a slovenly lubber is wounding a bird.

But if everything holds and your luck is still good
And you don't start to holler 'till you're out of the wood
You will slip round the bend in the creek and will see
Birds in their thousands as thick as can be.

And if they should stretch in a line by the water
And you get into range there is bound to be slaughter
Your heart beats too fast and your punt feels like lead
You get cramp in your neck and your fingers are dead.

You're too near in or you're too far out
And the devil is trying to spin you about
And now you're in range and the punt's moving fast
if the heads don't come up then the range will be past.

At last the ducks start and the lanyard's pulled back
Instead of a roar there's a dismal crack
The gun had misfired , you lie still and ache
With a pain in your hands as they slowly awake.

It seems suddenly cold and your tummy seems empty
You have nothing at all and you might have had plenty
Even the goose that you scorned on your way
Seems now the only chance of the day.

But after a pipe and a gentle blaspheme
You perk up a bit as the sun is now seen
You take a look at the sands and the bay
With their steely blue channels all stretching away.

There's bound to be duck, if not quite such a lot
For nothing's disturbed by powder and shot
And you feel yourself thankful, it's funny to say
For duck are still quarry when they fly away.

Gus Cockrell

In suitably poetic response here is **'The Ferryman's Reply':**

Dear Friend, your card with New Years Wishes
And lively tales of fowl and fishes
Has proved a winner for all time
Here's my acknowledgement in rhyme.

When you awoke that winters morn
And listened for the rain and storm
You little knew that by your bed
my spirit sat with upraised head
—and listened with you too

And when down to the creek you went
It's quiet footsteps with you bent
To float upon the tide
And down the reach where you espied
—that lonely old curlew

And when that single goose flew past
My spirits heart, like yours, beat fast
And ghostly hands reached for a gun
Then put it down when all was done
—for that's the thing to do

And when round the bend at last
With running tide, punt going fast
You sighted that good company
Of lively wigeon on a spree
—I smiled along with you

And now the glorious moment's come
The lanyards pulled—Oh damn the gun
The things my spirit said were rude
No self respecting spirit should
—be such a bawdy crew.

Then when the dawn broke o'er the bay
My poor old spirit stole away
For I was waking up in bed
And wouldn't like to have it said
—I'm spiritless, would you?

Very best wishes for 1950
Willie Hughes

I think these verses give some indication of the love which my father had for his sport, for the bay, for wild nature and for those who like him shared this wonderful common interest. He now rests in a grave in Kirkmabreck Churchyard in a lair specially selected by himself and my mother for its commanding view over 'The Inks', the Cree Estuary and Wigtown Bay where he spent some of the happiest days of his life. Some of his punting gear including the old muzzle loading puntgun 'Gus' can be seen in the Creetown Museum.

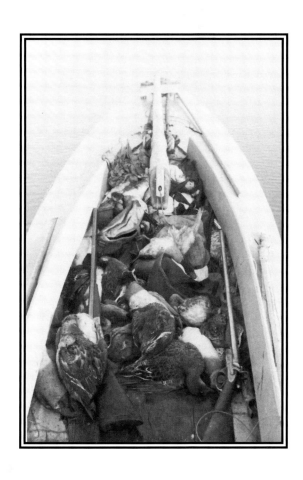

Adam Birrell before embarking for Gallipoli

Adam Birrell

One name which occurs in the ferryman stories and indeed in many books and articles about the Solway is that of Adam Birrell.

On a pleasant October morning I journeyed to Dumfries to meet Margaret Carrons one of Adams two daughters, who very kindly let me see the original Citation and medal that had been awarded to her father following the yachting tragedy off Auchencairn in 1909. Mr and Mrs Ferguson and their chauffeur Sidney Seal were drowned ; Adam and Captain Caird were the only survivors. A newspaper cutting of the time follows.

THE answer to the question "Who was Sidney Seal?" which landed on our desk last week was quickly supplied by Mr Drew Murray, who tells us that some of the older generation of Creetonians will remember Sidney Seal who was buried in Kirkmabreck Churchyard on 6th August 1909, aged 26 years. He was chauffeur to Mr and Mrs Ferguson, The Hill, Creetown, now known as Hill of Burns.

They were all drowned when on a boating outing in the Solway Firth. With them that day were Adam Birrell a local fisherman, and Captain Caird of Cassencary, who would be the grandfather of the present Laird. Their motor launch, "Sirius" went on fire off Auchencairn at the entrance to Balcary Bay. It was a beautiful warm day and the party were preparing to make tea on a paraffin stove when it went up in flames and exploded. In seconds the small cabin was ablaze and there was nothing for it but to abandon ship.

They were then between two and three miles off shore and, after seeing the other four in the water equipped with lifebelts, Adam Birrell set off to swim for help. At the end of a long struggle he reached Rascarrel Point completely exhausted and after climbing over rocks and running, falling and walking through woods and fields he contacted help at a farm house. Others were alerted and boats went out to try and rescue those in the sea, but two had disappeared and only two were picked up, one of whom died in the rescue boat.

Mr Birrell and Capt. Caird were the only survivors, the Fergusons and Sidney Seal lost their lives. They were buried in Kirkmabreck Churchyard, and while the stone marking the Ferguson graves is now difficult to read that of Sidney Seal is still fairly clear.

The picture of Sidney Seal's funeral can be found in some Creetown homes and it is something of a mystery that it should have been so recorded while there is no such record of the Ferguson's funeral. One can only assume that he was a member of the Creetown Territorials and they buried him with military honours. One of the pictures taken by Mr Charles Hunter, the photographer in the district in those days, shows a party of soldiers firing a salute over the grave.

It is also worth recording that Mr Birrell, who commanded the Territorials. was born in Carsluith but lived almost all his life in Creetown. He was later awarded the Royal Humane Society Medal for Bravery.

Adam always lived in Creetown and was nearly 91 when he died. He and his brother Willie ran the two salmon fisheries at Creetown and Carsluith. A major Hulse from Bude in Cornwall came to shoot with Adam and stayed in the Barholme Hotel in the town. It was he who was responsible for getting Adam interested in Punt Gunning and together they built two craft. Adam then shot as a hobby in the winter around Creetown and at Glencaple below Annan. The salmon season ran from February until September which left the winter free for shooting. Salmon caught were stored in the fish house and then sent to Billingsgate market in London.

At the outbreak of the first world war, Adam who was already in the Territorial Army was called up and sent to Gallipoli with the Kings Own Scottish Borderers. He received a head wound and was transferred to Egypt to recover and served the rest of the war there. During this time he developed an interest in archaeology which in later years saw him become vice-president of the Dumfries and Galloway Society.

Also in later years he found time to take people out punting and among those he helped was a young student from Cambridge University who had been sent by an uncle; the student was Peter Scott.

James Robertson Justice also shot with Adam. He was just starting his film career and offered Adam a small part in a picture called The Brothers which was being shot near the Isle of Skye. Adam was unfortunately injured while there and did not therefore appear.

For further references see:
The Solway Firth by Brian Blake
Wildfowlers and Fishermen on the Solway by Wally Wright.

SATURDAY ADVENTURE

by Ferryman

everything seemed set for the shot of a lifetime

TO begin with it certainly was not the best time of day to set out on a punting expedition, "but needs must when the devil drives" and work having to come first, a Saturday afternoon outing was at least better than nothing. Thus it came about that, after a hurried lunch, I launched the single punt, loaded the big muzzle-loading punt gun, dumped my gear aboard and rowed off down our mooring creek towards the river. The river is a tidal one, its waters reaching the sea through a number of channels flanked by mudbanks in the upper tidal reaches, and sandbanks in the lower. Here and there smaller streams join the river in the estuary, and a couple of miles or sobelow our mooring creek it is joined by the main tributary, a small river much favoured by duck and sometimes the home of large numbers of wigeon and teal. Close to the mouth of our mooring creek is The Gut, another favoured duck haunt, but apart from some curlew and one or two oyster-catchers The Gut was empty.

The main river proved little better and so far as I could see contained only a few shoveler near the mouth of the tributary. Although I had no intention of shooting at these birds I lay down and "set" the punt to them in order that I might have a close-up of their remarkable feeding activities, an operation that never failed to interest me. Having without much difficulty got close enough for the purpose, I got out the glasses to watch the shoveler. These birds, about 30 in number, were swimming round in circles in very shallow water, the circles getting smaller and smaller until the birds were packed into what appeared like a solid mass. Suddenly they shot apart and commenced feeding, this operation being accompanied by a spluttering sound as their great beaks filtered from the muddy water the small creatures their combined efforts had disturbed.

Having in my absorbed interest allowed the punt to drift too close, the shoveler spotted me and with their characteristically loud wing beats, took off, and flying round behind me, pitched into the river some distance away. Standing up in the punt I examined through the glasses all the likely spots in the vicinity where duck might be found, but apart from the little flotilla of shoveler and one or two pintail sitting on the banks of the tributary, the place was as bare as Mother Hubbard's cupboard. While I speculated upon whether or not to proceed any farther, I caught sight of a great mass of birds milling around, a couple of miles or so down the estuary. Even though they were a long way off they had the look of duck, and the binocular revealed them to be wigeon, a veritable cloud, and presently they pitched on the edge of the main channel just where, at this state of the tide, it reached the open sea. Ordinarily the sight of these birds would have sent me off without delay, but this was a period of neap tides and consequently of poor ebbs. Even at dead low tide the great protecting sandbanks would be covered by many feet of water, and the recent gales had left behind a legacy in the form of an "old sea" resulting in a big swell. My little punt with its five inches of freeboard enjoyed my full confidence, but it had its limitations ! Again I picked up the glasses.

It was a day of blue skies across which patches of cloud sailed like argosies before the fresh breeze. Out in the bay the water was white-capped and even in the channel mouth the swell broke on the sandbank upon which the wigeon were sitting. I looked long and carefully while a jumble of thoughts passed through my mind—"What a fine lot they were—if I thought there was a reasonable chance I might risk it—pity about that surf though, sure to be nasty down there—too nasty. . . ." If the wigeon had not moved at that moment I think I would have decided not to attempt a stalk, but they did move! I watched them avidly. After flying around for a short time they again pitched on the sandbank, this time a little closer. The sight of this tremendous company challenged my caution and better judgement. I racked my brain for excuses....

The wigeon had moved at least twice already in the last half hour; I reasoned, might they not move again and this time pitch closer, perhaps even far enough up channel to be clear of the breaking seas? If I waited any longer where I was there would be no hope whatsoever of getting near them as the flood tide would soon be setting in. In any case the surf might not be anything like as bad as it looked through the glasses, and I could always turn back if it became nasty, couldn't I ? Pushing my doubts into the back of my mind I got out the setting pole without further ado and, kneeling in the stern of the punt, commenced the long stalk. For the first mile or so I made rapid progress, the strong current hurrying the punt along despite the fresh head wind. The bottom of the channel was of firm sand and the setting-pole hissed through the water in the forward movement of each lusty stroke. As the distance from the duck shortened I got down on my left elbow and pushed on at my best speed, occasionally taking a glance ahead. The punt was now beginning to feel the effect of the swell, but at this stage it was nothing to worry about, and I continued to make good progress. When about half-a-mile from the wigeon I lay down flat on my face and the most difficult stage of the stalk began.

The wigeon were sitting on a sandbank on the seaward side of a wide creek which debouched into the main channel at this point. The outflow of water from the creek had created a sandy spit which curved out into the channel and which was acting as a sort of breakwater. Unfortunately it appeared likely that it would be necessary to circumnavigate this spit in order to get within range of the duck. This was a formidable obstacle. By keeping as far off shore as possible (which, as the bank shelved quite steeply, was actually only a short distance), I contrived to reach the spit without shipping more than a gallon of water, which splashed over the side as the swell tilted the punt in passing. I now paused briefly to consider the best way in which to tackle the spit, the noise of the breaking sea having left me in no doubt that the operation would be fraught with some risk. Raising my head with infinite caution I peeped past the side of the gun and my heart sank; a great curling sea raced toward the spit and broke on the seaward side with a crash and flurry of foam—if the punt had been there at that moment, well—I shuddered.

Edging the punt round a little until the gun was bearing right on the duck, I took a quick look in their direction, my heart missed a beat and the old excitement gripped me. They were much closer than I had thought, within long range, in fact. Oh . . . ! if only they had been just a little closer I wouldn't have had to worry about the spit. Well ... why should I worry about it...? Certainly they were rather far away, but even so I ought to be able to knock over a good number from that lot. I cocked the action of the gun and put my left hand on the stock, easing the weight of the muzzle off the rest. With the setting-pole in my right hand I edged the punt forward until her bow touched the sand—this was as close as I could get. Cautiously I raised my head and looked along the gun. They were a wonderful sight. The sight of a lifetime ! More than two thousand wigeon were there, stretching along the sandbank in a dense mass. Never had I seen a chance like this.... My right hand released the setting-pole (which was fastened to the punt by a length of cord) and seized the lanyard. My mind raced ahead . . . the gun was pointing right down the dense ranks of the wigeon, it was inconceivable that even a single pellet would go astray ... if I fired now from this angle and at this range I would inevitably wound a large number of duck, some at least of which would swim out to sea where I would be unable to pursue them in the rough water.

Well, that was a pity, but it couldn't be helped and even so this would be my record shot, that was for sure ! I pressed down on the stock, bringing the muzzle of the gun to the correct elevation. A doubt nagged at my conscience—they were rather far away, the muzzle was higher than it ought to be for a normal shot at sitting birds. For an instant of time selfishness fought with reason and reason won. I couldn't do it ! Releasing the lanyard I eased back down into the bottom of the punt, at the same time lowering the gun on to the rest. I would have to get closer ... much closer. My hand groped for the setting-pole. I would try to weather the spit. Working the punt backward until I had plenty of " sea room," an operation of considerable difficulty, I approached the spit at such an angle as would show as little as possible of the punt to the still unsuspecting duck. Unfortunately this had the effect of laying the punt almost beam on to the sea, but I noticed as I approached, that after a particularly big wave had broken, a brief lull usually occurred during which the swells were much smaller and only broke at the moment of impact.

Watching my chance I hung back until a big wave had crashed down on the spit and receded in a smother of foam, then using every ounce of energy I shot the punt forward. Nothing venture, nothing win ! The punt surged forward past the tip of the spit, violently rocked by several successive swells but shipping only a little water. A few moments later I glanced to my right front over the edge of the roaming. The nearest birds were now within easy range, but the powerful backwash had caused the punt's head to fall off to seaward and the gun would not bear. In an anguish of dread lest the duck should jump me at the last moment, I worked like fury striving to push the stern of the punt outward against the persistent undertow. I was within an ace of making a fantastic shot. A tremendous excitement gripped me and the sweat poured down my cheeks as I shoved away, forgetting everything else. Suddenly the sky seemed to darken and the punt was thrown violently sideways. I glanced over my left shoulder ; a curling wall of water appeared to hover momentarily over the punt. Where it thinned at its white-tipped crest I could see, as through thick glass, the blue of the sky subtly changed to green. It dropped with stunning force on my back, knocking all the air out of my lungs and swamping the punt instantly ! The next few moments are only a confused memory.

Eventually I found myself standing chest deep in the water, endeavouring to prevent the punt capsizing and dumping all my gear into the sea. Because of the air trapped under her long foredeck, the punt remained awash instead of sinking like a stone, and by "walking" her along I succeeded in getting her back into the comparative shelter of the sand spit. There I was faced with the problem of getting the water out of her, a very difficult matter indeed, since no matter how hard I baled, each succeeding wave filled her to the brim. In the end I got over this by pulling the punt ashore, unlashing the breeching rope and laying the gun in the bottom of the cockpit, thus lowering the punt's centre of gravity. I then swam her out far enough to be clear of the breaking waves and, while she wallowed at anchor, I hung on alongside and baled until she was sufficiently buoyant to allow me to climb aboard. Having accomplished this with some difficulty, it was only a matter of time until the punt was baled dry, the mast stepped, the sodden sail hoisted and, with a fair wind and the now flowing tide, I pulled up the anchor and set out for home.

The rest of the tale is easily told except for one thing.... Oh yes, I made it all right, soaked to the skin, of course, with the cold kept at bay by dint of hard work with the paddle I used to urge the punt along as well as to steer. I expect, however, you will be wondering what happened to the duck . . . how did they react to this catastrophe ? Just when did they go ? I have never ceased to wonder.

11

A Day to Remember

Ferryman remembers his first goose shot under Arctic conditions

ALTHOUGH it all took place a very long time ago, I can remember each incident as clearly as though it had happened only yesterday, for it was, indeed, a day to remember—it was the day I shot my first goose. Oh, yes, I know that innumerable "first goose" stories have been told and retold, but my goose was different. Not only was it the first of its kind, but it was also the last, for out of the hundreds of geese I subsequently shot, not one other of this species came my way.

During the night the snow had fallen heavily and the gale-force wind had piled it into deep drifts. By early morning, although the blizzard had somewhat abated, it was still much too severe to permit me to carry out my intention of being out on the merse at first light. Daylight came reluctantly as I fumed and fretted and still the snow fell, and it was well on in the forenoon before I was able to set out, muffled like an eskimo and wearing over everything else a shopkeeper's old white coat to act as camouflage. On top of my grey balaclava I wore a white cover from an old service cap, and there is little doubt that these make-shift items served their purpose well. When I reached it, the merse bore a close resemblance to the Arctic tundra. It was completely snowbound, the neap tide during the night having been nowhere near the grass, and was being swept by sheets of drift snow, small and crystalline, which stung any exposed skin like lead shot. Most of the smaller creeks were already snow-filled or covered by snow bridges and only the larger and deeper creeks were visible.

Because of this it was necessary to walk warily, but I was on my own ground in a manner of speaking and knew this part of the merse like the palm of my hand, so I had little difficulty in avoiding trouble. With the wind behind me I made good progress, each successive gust hurrying me along while the drift rattled like sand on my back. Scarcely a blade of grass was to be seen, and these only on the edge of some of the deeper creeks where the wind had blown the snow clear. I decided to take cover in one such creek where a thin stubble of grass fringed the edge like a badly shaven chin. Standing with my back to the wind I was somewhat protected by the bank on the windward side. Visibility in any direction was very restricted and was confined to looking across or down wind, as any attempt to look into the wind resulted in one being temporarily blinded by the stinging drift. I was hopeful that some of the wigeon, which were unlikely to have been able to feed during the night, would come looking for any grass that was showing, nor was I disappointed, for I had hardly settled in when three of these birds appeared like ghosts out of the murk, and one fell to the shot from my single-barrelled gun. This gun, the only one I then possessed, was my pride and joy. A cheap single 12-bore 'Knoxall', I had bought it the previous autumn from a firm in Newington Butts with my carefully hoarded pocket money. Since my father had refused point blank to allow me to use it without a gun licence, I had been compelled to wait for several weeks while the necessary 10s. was forthcoming. A loan from my brother provided a box of cartridges and we had subsequently enjoyed modest sport with it. I still have this old gun and, although it is seldom used now, in its time it has accounted for a great many wildfowl of all kinds.

Having picked up my wigeon, I set it up on the creek edge to act as a decoy, fixing it in place with pieces of wire brought for that very purpose. A long wait followed, during which I was forced several times to crouch down in the creek bottom while I rubbed my nearly frozen face to restore the circulation. It was one of these occasions which caused me to miss my chance at the greylag. I had put the gun down on the creek edge in order to free both hands and was busily chafing away when I thought I heard a goose. Straightening up I was just in time to see about 20 greylag vanishing into the murk, visibility at that time being little more than a long gunshot. These birds must have passed quite close to me unseen and unheard in the tumult. Disappointed, I renewed my vigilance, determined. that this would not happen again —but it very nearly did.

Forced by the intense cold to seek a short respite by crouching in the creek bottom, I straightened up just in time to catch a small party of wigeon apparently about to pitch beside my decoy. My shot caught them a yard or so above the ground and to my joy three fell to the snow. These were quickly retrieved and set up with the others. Two were drakes in magnificent plumage and I remember to this day how I gloated over them as I set them up as life-like as possible. This was marvellous, never before had I shot three duck with one shot. Glory be ! . . . two shots and four duck down I could hardly believe it. Agog with excitement I renewed my watch, my head turning from side to side like a spectator at a tennis match. Once or twice I caught a fleeting glimpse of duck, but always they had gone before I could get the gun to my shoulder.

Suddenly five large birds loomed out of the drift, flying straight up wind and a little to my left. In a twinkling I had lined up on the nearest and had almost pressed the trigger when I realised they were sheldduck. I lowered the gun— good job I had spotted them in time, not only would I have been shooting at a protected bird, but I would have wasted a precious cartridge ! I felt in my pocket, counting the cartridges with my fingers—seven, and one in the gun—only eight left. Yes, a good job that, I would have to watch out !

Some time later another little party of wigeon appeared and, ignoring my decoys, flew along the line of the creek in which I was concealed. Visibility having by then improved considerably I was able to watch the wigeon for some distance and I got the impression they had pitched either in or near the creek. Being extremely cold I decided to attempt a stalk in the hope of warming myself up a bit. I had little hope of getting a shot at the duck as the creek was blocked with snow almost to the top in places, but anyhow I could try. The stalk proved as difficult as I had foreseen, but I was young and fit and thought nothing of worming along on my belly where the snow drifts nearly filled the creek, the main difficulty being to prevent the gun-barrel becoming blocked with snow. On reaching, as near as I could guess, the point at which I had lost sight of the duck, I cautiously raised my head and looked along the creek. I could not have judged it better —they were there all right, about a dozen wigeon, feeding on the fringe of grass along the creek edge. A little group of three immediately caught my eye. Aiming carefully I waiting until their heads came up and fired. They never moved from the spot.

Hardly believing my good luck I climbed out of the creek and rushed along to retrieve my prizes. They lay on the snowy grass in a little line—a hen and two more beautiful cock wigeon. I was beside myself with joy. Three shots seven wigeon! I danced around in the snow in sheer exuberance. Picking up the duck I returned to my original position and, after making sure no snow had got into the barrel, reloaded the gun. Suddenly I felt ravenously hungry and decided to wait only about another half-hour after which I would pack up and go home. I looked forward to this homecoming; my mother had not been very keen on my setting out in the snow but I knew she would be delighted by the success of my venture and I could hardly wait to show her my bag.

After a time, having seen nothing more, I collected the wigeon I had set up as decoys; they were as hard as boards and frozen into the shape into which I had set them. Placing them in the bag with the others I was about to sling it over my shoulder when I spotted a large bird flying in my direction. Hastily sliding back into the creek I watched it carefully. It looked very large and at first I thought it might be a cormorant, but as it drew nearer I realised it was a goose. A moment or two later it passed on my right at a range of about 40 yards. Closing one eye I aimed at its head as with a rifle, jerked the muzzle ahead a little and fired; to my unspeakable joy the goose plummeted to the ground stone dead. For a moment, astonishment at my unheard of success held me rigid, and then I was out of the creek like a shot and rushing across to where the goose lay in the snow. Picking it up I brushed the snow from its feathers with my hand; a stain of blood marked the spot where its head had lain. My triumph was complete !

I looked at my prize with interest, for it was smaller than I had thought and lighter. Dark above and light below, the head, neck and chest were black except for a little white "half collar" on the neck. I thought it might be a brent. Later that evening, following my triumphant home-coming, I took my goose round to the old expert for positive identification. There was really no need to do this as the picture and description in my bird book left little doubt about the species, but I just could not resist the temptation to display my prize to the great man. Ushered by his wife into his den, where a roaring stove glowed red hot, I explained my errand and held out the goose. Donning a pair of spectacles, the expert examined the bird. "Where did you say you shot this ?" he asked. I told him. "Aye, aye, it's a brent, ye ken, a most unusual bird for this district —must have got lost in the storm—weel, weel, fancy that." "Have you ever seen one here before ?" I asked. "Aye, I have that," he replied, "but only once. About 25 years ago my brother shot one out of a little bunch of five not very far from where you shot this one." He nodded, "I wouldn't be surprised if it was another 25 before another one turns up."

He was right up to a point; 25 years have come and gone and the better part of another 25, and so far as I know my brent was the last of its kind to visit us.

......a large bird flying in my direction.......   Noel Dudley

13

Tit *for* Tat

Noel Dudley

Ferryman describes a morning when the geese were on the move

THE geese were late in flighting that morning, and it was almost daylight when the first wavering line approached up-river from the direction of the sands, battling the strong and bitter head-wind, and silhouetted against the sunrise like a Peter Scott painting.

Straining our ears we listened for the first sounds of " goose music," and soon, in spite of the wind and the noise of the small surf breaking along the river's edge, we heard the first faint notes, that, as always, set our hearts beating faster, and banished all thoughts of cold and discomfort. The prospects were good, for we had heard the geese flying along this flight-line on the two previous mornings, and in the faint light of dawn had caught a glimpse of the great birds as they passed over our heads on their way inland. On these mornings not a breath of wind had ruffled the tide, and the geese, high above the reach of our guns, had passed unmolested to their feeding grounds. Now the odds were in our favour if the geese used the same flight-line, and there was no reason to suppose they would not, they would have to face a strong head-wind, and would, we hoped, be low enough for a shot.

As the light strengthened, our anticipation grew more acute, and we strained our eyes into the distance. More than once our pulses quickened as a dimly seen line of birds became visible, but always they turned out to be curlew or gulls moving up from the sands. We became uneasy . . . yesterday and the day before they were here long before this . .. if they were going to come at all they would have to come soon . . . surely they were not going to let us down today, now that we had the wind just right. As these thoughts passed through my mind a distant line of birds caught my eye; this time there could be no mistake.

" Bob," I shouted, pointing. "Geese."

" Aye, I see them," he replied, " now mind, if they come over us keep your head down until the last second."

" Yes, righto," I replied, " will do." The distant line wavered and flickered, rising and falling a little as the geese forged ahead against the wind. We watched anxiously; they certainly looked good; they were well within range of the ground and if they kept to their present course we could hardly fail to get a shot.

As always, I felt a tremendous excitement welling up inside me . . . goose fever. . . . I crouched in the creek like a coiled spring. Now we could hear their voices faintly, but unmistakably . . . greylag. . . . I listened, straining my ears, trying to judge their position from the sound. As the clamour grew louder I could stand it no longer and risked a peep through the grass blades fringing the creek. They were almost up to us, barely 30 yards high. My heart beat like a sledge-hammer and I trembled with excitement. The geese were a little to my right and were going to pass right over Bob as he crouched in the creek about 20 yards away. The goose music reached a crescendo and they swept overhead. At that instant Bob stood up and I followed suit; the entire skein shot upward, their forward progress momentarily arrested. As I swung on the goose at the end of the line I heard Bob's gun go off twice, and out of the tail of my eye saw one goose drop like a stone and another, obviously hard hit, turn out of the skein and blow away to leeward. My own shot brought the nearest goose crashing down behind us and my second dropped another.

While Bob collected all three dead birds I snatched out my binocular and watched his second bird, which was rapidly losing height as it flew with the wind behind it obliquely over the river. Clearing the further bank by only a few feet, the the goose flopped down on the merse and almost at once a man, of whose presence we had been quite unaware, emerged from a nearby creek and, hastening across, picked up the goose, which appeared to be dead, or almost so. A second person then appeared on the scene, and since there was no boat available with which to cross the river, we watched helplessly while they debated this "gift from the gods." After a few moments conversation the man who had picked up the goose walked to the river bank, held up the goose and, looking in our direction, swung it pendulum fashion a few times, then, laying down the goose and his gun, spread out his arms in a gesture of helplessness which plainly said, " Sorry, chaps, but there is nothing I can do about it."

14

After briefly bewailing the loss of our goose and consoling ourselves that at least someone had benefited, we decided to " give it another hour " and returned to our former positions. The two gunners on the opposite side of the river did likewise, and about half-an-hour later a large skein appeared from seaward coming in our direction and flying at no great height. This skein was spread out over a wide front and it appeared inevitable that part of it would pass within range of the hidden gunners, who, as well as being on our right, were well to our front. Sure enough, the skein suddenly lifted skyward, and in the same instant two geese plummeted to the ground. The thud of four shots reached us and a third goose, hard hit, began losing height as it struggled vainly to keep up with the rest of the skein, which had now climbed out of shot. The surviving, geese, with a mighty clamour, passed straight over our heads on their way inland, and our attention was centred on the wounded bird which, now down to a height of a few yards, had given up the struggle against the wind and was crossing our front a considerable distance away.

Suddenly the goose folded up and dropped like a stone. With a whoop of glee Bob was out of the creek in a trice and splashing across the merse as fast as he could go. With gun at the ready he approached the goose, which had fallen into a water-filled " puddle " on the merse, but no "coup de grace" was necessary—the goose was stone dead. With a wide grin on his face, Bob came panting back to where I was standing on the creek bank.

" Well, what do you think of that ? " he exclaimed, holding up the goose—a fine grey-lag, " nobody will ever believe this."

" Except the two chaps over the river," I replied. " I wonder who the devil they are ? "

" Goodness knows," said Bob, " but they have certainly paid us back for our lost goose."

We both turned in the direction of our friends, who were standing in full view and one of whom was watching us through a pair of binoculars. Holding aloft the goose, Bob swung it to and fro. An answering wave from our friends indicated that they fully understood the situation, and were no doubt as astonished as we at the almost incredible outcome of our " combined operation." Shortly afterwards, having packed our gear, we turned to leave. I glanced across the river; our friends were moving off, too. With a final wave we went our separate ways; we were in great spirits—I expect they were also.

" Tit had been returned for Tat." Honour was satisfied.

THE PLAN

Noel Dudley

*it was a good one,
remembers Ferryman, and
should have worked, but . . .*

AS we launched the punt in the early morning dark we were not without some slight misgivings, but these were quickly routed by the supreme confidence and enthusiasm of youth. Besides, had we not waited patiently for the opportunity we knew awaited us out there in the dark? For some time past we had been aware of a great mass of wigeon flighting down the sands at first light into a certain tidal reach of the tributary that joined our main river in the estuary about two miles below our moorings. We had decided to wait until low tide coincided with first light, so that the duck would be concentrated in the smallest possible area, thus increasing the chances of pulling off a " big shot ".

The chosen morning had arrived and nothing would stop us carrying out our plan of attack. This was to pull up the tributary to a point well above the reach into which we expected the wigeon to pitch, wait until they were all ashore, and drop down on them at full speed with the aid of the current. It was a good plan—simple in detail, as all good plans should be—and ought to have succeeded—but it didn't!

Arriving at the mouth of the tributary in the intense darkness of pre-dawn, we found the current coming down with such force that we were compelled to ship the oars and resort to poling upstream as close to the water's edge as the punt would float. With the wind also against us this operation took all our youthful skill and strength. It was still dark, and with the tide falling rapidly we decided to move out into the stream and anchor, rather than lie alongside the bank where the punt might have gone aground. Standing amidships, my companion, Bob, with a thrust of the setting-pole, pushed the punt out into the stream, and when he gave the word I dropped the grapnel over the stern. Turning, I sat down on the stern seat, and Bob, who was still standing holding the setting-pole, also turned to sit down. At that precise moment the punt reached the end of the anchor rope and stopped dead. Caught off balance, Bob, with a wild cry, threw his arms in the air, hurling the setting-pole into the darkness, and shot past me over the side of the punt. At the last instant I made a frantic sweep with both arms and found myself clutching one of his legs encased in a long rubber boot. Hampered by the thick mittens I wore, I was unable to get a proper grip on the slippery rubber, and only by pressing the boot against my chest was I able to prevent him being swept away by the swift current. Our combined weight, and the terrific pull of the current on Bob's body caused the punt to heel over to such an extent that the water poured over the gunwale, and it was with great relief that I dimly discerned a hand emerge from the water and grip the gunwale. Letting go Bob's leg I tore off my mitts and gripping his wrist, with a mighty heave, soon had him lying gasping across the cockpit.

Soaked to the skin, but otherwise none the worse for his immersion, Bob immediately commenced baling out the dangerous amount of water we had shipped, working at top speed in an attempt to keep some heat in his rapidly chilling body. It was obvious that if Bob was to escape serious exposure we would have to reach a place of shelter as soon as possible, so the instant we deemed it safe to do so I commenced hauling on the anchor rope. That we had misjudged the strength of the current now became more apparent. As soon as about two-thirds of the rope was aboard and the angle of pull had become sufficiently acute, the stern of the punt began to " bore " into the river and again the water came pouring in. I released the rope in haste, and the water-logged punt dropped back to her original position. Once again we baled her dry and made another attempt to get the anchor up, but the result was exactly as before. Since the situation was getting serious we decided to cut the anchor rope, only to discover that neither of us had a knife in our possession! By now Bob was almost frozen with cold, so stripping off his soaked jersey, shirt and underclothing, I dressed him in my own jersey and punting coat. This was a slight improvement, but it was desperately urgent that we got under way as quickly as possible, so getting Bob to lie along the gun-deck, in order to have as much weight as possible forward, I gripped the anchor rope once again. Pulling it slowly and cautiously I worked the punt towards the anchor. This time I got closer than before, but again the stern of the punt began to "bore" and the water flooded in. Frantically I hauled on the rope and suddenly the sound of water pouring into the punt ceased. In the silence that followed a wave of relief passed over me—the grapnel had pulled clear—we were under way at last.

Getting out the oars we rowed down the tributary at a great pace, dawn was breaking, and the whee-oos of wigeon could be heard as the first small companies arrived, but we gave little thought to these. Arriving in the main river, we were faced by a two-mile row against the swollen stream and the last of the ebb tide. This we accomplished by stepping the mast, hoisting our small lug-sail and creeping up-stream as close to the bank as possible, using our setting-poles both to push and to steer. Since it was impossible to enter our mooring creek until the tide returned, we anchored the punt in the river, and carrying our guns and some of our sodden gear, plodded wearily homewards. As we squelched across the merse Bob turned to me, " Well, old boy, I don't know what you think, but I reckon I'll give this game up, it's too darned tough for me." I nodded in agreement, " me, too."

At half-past-five the following morning we dropped down river under a cloudless sky, bright with stars. A vagrant breeze scarcely ruffled the water, and above the sigh of the tide only the squeak of the rollocks and the splash of the oars disturbed the quiet of the morning. The punt was clean and dry, we had seen to that the previous afternoon. The puntgun shells were freshly loaded, the cripple-stopper tin was filled to the brim with green "Primax" cartridges, new and shiny. We were warm and dry. We were young and excited and happy. There was still a fair amount of water coming down the tributary, but nothing like the flood we had encountered the previous morning. We shipped the oars and started to push upstream. Our plan was unchanged; it was a good plan, and it ought to work.

The sack of wigeon we carried home later that day proved that this time it did!

Unforeseen Hazard

recalled by Ferryman

Noel Dudley

The only hope was the giant log . . .

IT seems to me, after a lifetime's experience, that a pre-requisite to safety in wildfowling is a thorough knowledge of the tides, winds, fogs, muds, creeks, etc., of the locality in which one proposes to shoot. If one does not already possess this knowledge, then one should always be accompanied by someone who does. If an unforeseeable emergency then arises, the chances of coming out of it alive and well are greatly enhanced.

The truth of the foregoing is, I think, clearly indicated in the following account of an incident in which I was involved many, many years ago. As our threesome approached the cattle-bridge that memorable morning, leaning into the wind that swept at gale force across the merse, we had little inkling of the danger we were to meet and narrowly survive. The bridge spanned the Judge's burn, a deep, wide and treacherous creek barring the approaches to the merse at this point. To be sure, we were well aware that the great spring tide which would soon be racing up the Bay would cover the bridge and the entire merse. My brother Jack and I had also pointed out to our less experienced friend Hugh, that the howling south-easter would undoubtedly produce an abnormally high tide, and it was essential that we got off the merse in good time.

Before we separated at the cattle-bridge, each to his chosen place, I, the eldest of the trio, both in years and experience, reminded the others that as soon as I gave the signal we must foregather at the bridge, and leave the merse in a body. Hugh, who was armed with a mighty double-barrelled 8-bore, elected to go right out to the merse edge in the hope of getting a shot at some of the duck we confidently expected to be dislodged from their resting grounds by the raging sea. Jack and I each chose a position nearer the middle of the merse where we thought we stood a good chance of a shot, not only at duck, but perhaps at geese as well. As the tide began to race up the estuary the anticipated movement began, and large numbers of duck could be seen flying backwards and forwards along the tide's edge. Later, as the tide advanced towards the merse small parties of these would, from time to time, come right in over the grass, and now and again the boom of Hugh's 8-bore would be carried to us on the gale. Soon we were all enjoying good sport, and the temptation to hang on until the last minute had to be resisted.

When I judged the time had come to move off the merse, I stood up and waved, as had been arranged. Immediately Jack got out of the creek in which he had been concealed, and began making his way towards the cattle-bridge, a considerable distance off. Facing the direction of Hugh's hideout I continued to wave until, finally, his figure emerged from the creek and stood silhouetted against the foaming breakers which now filled the entire bay. Satisfied that all was well, I made my way towards our rendezvous, the wind in my back pushing me along like a giant hand. On nearing the bridge our converging courses brought my brother and I together, and we both stopped and looked back to see what progress our friend was making. To our intense alarm not a sign of him could we see. Hoping that perhaps an approaching party of duck had induced him to take temporary cover, we both began waving urgently, and finally, after a few anxious minutes we saw to our great relief, his head and shoulders emerge from a creek. Our relief was short lived however, for he appeared to be unwilling or unable to leave the creek. We renewed our urgent waving and shouted uselessly into the teeth of the gale. At last we saw him crawl over the edge of the creek, slowly, leaning on the butt of his gun, he stood up, took a few faltering steps and fell flat on his face ! We now knew beyond any shadow of doubt what we had feared all along—our friend was either injured or ill and was in immediate need of assistance. To say that we were seriously worried is to put it mildly ! We looked at the cattle-bridge—the water was almost up to the boards. If we were going to get off the merse it would have to be within the next few minutes.

I looked at Jack. " You understand that by the time we get Hugh to the bridge there will be no hope of any of us getting off the merse ? " Jack nodded, " Well, it can't be helped, let's go and get him ! "

Not very far from the bridge a huge log, brought in by a previous high tide, had become grounded on top of what remained of an old turf bank, that at one time flanked the entire length of the Judge's burn on the seaward side. I pointed to the log, " That is our only chance, if we can get there and the log stays put, we should be able to last out the tide". We hurried across to the log, stacked our guns and gear on top of it, and then at a jog trot set out across the merse. As we neared our friend we could see him making desperate efforts to reach us, staggering and falling repeatedly, but still dragging his heavy gun, and a string of seven pintail he had shot.

On reaching him we discovered he had developed an acute attack of asthma, which made it almost impossible for him to breathe. Poor Hugh, his mobility was reduced to a few steps at a time with a long rest between, while he struggled and fought for breath. After a brief rest and concealing our concern from him as best we could, we set off on the return journey, half walking and half dragging him across the merse. We found the best method of making progress was to place Hugh between us with an arm over each of our shoulders. In this way we could slide him along when he was unable to walk, but it was exhausting work as Hugh was a hefty chap, taller than either Jack or I. Since he had shown great distress when we had proposed leaving his gun (a borrowed one) behind, I carried it along by its strap over my shoulder while Jack took charge of the duck.

To begin with we made fair progress, our knowledge of the merse enabling us to avoid the deepest of the creeks, now rapidly filling as the tide swept in behind us. Soon, however, the water spilled over the edges and in a few minutes we were struggling along in a sea of muddy water with nothing now to indicate the positions of the many creeks we still had to negotiate. From then on the journey was a hideous nightmare of plunging slowly along through the freezing and ever-deepening water, of stepping over the edge of unseen creeks, fortunately most of them narrow, and floundering out again on the other side, of Hugh's exhortations to leave him and look after ourselves, of fending off great sheets of ice that had floated out of the multitude of frozen flashes on the merse, and of the slap of water on our backs as the depth increased and the sea built up. Ahead of us nothing could now be seen of the merse except the great log, and the tops of the fence posts flanking the bridge. Slowly we struggled nearer our haven of refuge; we were almost spent, our water-filled sea-boots seemed weighted with lead and every step was a victory over deadly fatigue. I was desperately worried not only about Hugh but about my brother who was by no means as tough as myself. If I was at my last gasp what must he be like ? A great fear gripped me and I fought despair as well as fatigue. Ever more slowly we plunged along. I had now to support almost all of Hugh's weight as Jack could do no more, and then, quite suddenly, there was the log only a few yards away....

We reached it in a state of utter exhaustion. Gasping for breath we leaned against the log, standing in the water that now beat against the lower part. After a time, having somewhat recovered, we boosted Hugh on to the top of the log and after adding his gun and the duck to the pile of gear already there, Jack and I climbed wearily aboard. It now became apparent that our survival depended almost entirely upon whether or not the tide washed the log off the bank. We had reached the end of our strength and could have done little to save ourselves, had this occurred. Shivering uncontrollably as the bitter wind tore through our sodden clothing we watched anxiously as the tide rose. By now the merse, as we had foreseen, was a sea of raging water, dotted with jagged ice floes. Great sheets of spindrift lashed us and the paralysing cold crept into our bones. Poor Hugh was in the depth of despair, and kept blaming himself for our predicament. Fortunately, his breathing had improved somewhat, but he was in a serious state and we were desperately anxious about him.

Gradually the force of the waves beating against our refuge increased, and despite our combined weight a noticeable movement could be felt. We clung on desperately as the log rocked to and fro, hoping against hope that the tide would turn before it was driven off the bank by the breaking seas. Above the roar of the wind and sea a new sound now became audible. . . . Geese . . . Their voices sounded almost in our ears. We looked round. . . . They were passing close by on the seaward side.... A skein of grey-lag, flying across the wind, and only a few feet above the water. I wondered if they portended good or evil....

After what seemed an eternity, but could only have been a relatively short time, the movements of the log became less pronounced, and soon, to our great relief, they almost ceased.... The tide had turned. Then came the long wait in the bitter cold until the tide had retreated sufficiently to allow us to get off the merse. As soon as it was possible to do so we slid from our perch, and huddling close together took shelter from the wind in the lee of the log. During this wait Hugh's breathing had improved to a remarkable extent, and in spite of our frozen condition, our spirits rose with the falling tide, so that when the time came we stumbled across the bridge and shoreward, carrying all our gear and all our birds; nothing was left behind.

In due course we sat, all three of us, our knees up to our chins, in the huge old-fashioned bath in Hugh's house. The warm water laved our near frozen bodies, a delicious lassitude stole over us. . . . It was glorious. We listened to the wind howling outside the bathroom window and solemnly agreed it must be rather chilly out on the merse. We laughed a lot and thought the world a very fine place. Two days later when I visited the scene of our adventure, the great log had vanished", and I never saw it again.

Wild Goose Chase

Ferryman attempts to get a goose for a friend

...Seconds later two shots rang out in quick succession...

Noel Dudley

WHEN I answered the knock at the door and found H. standing on the threshold, the inevitable cigarette glowing in the dark, I had a feeling that once again interesting, and perhaps exciting, times lay ahead. H was that kind of chap. Things happened to him ! He was, he informed me, determined to shoot at least one goose during this leave, and could I possibly take him out the following morning ? I could and I would. As luck would have it, I myself had three days " off the chain " and these had been earmarked for an attack on the geese.

Thus it came about that next morning, in inky darkness and lashing rain, we rowed across the river, a strong wind opposed to the ebbing tide creating a nasty sea that was just about all our little boat could manage. Having landed safely and rather thankfully on the other side, we anchored the boat and unloaded our gear, preparatory to setting out across the merse to the point where we hoped to intercept the geese as they flighted off the sands at first light. H. volunteered to carry the game-bag in which was packed our food and thermos flasks; it also contained our spare cartridges, which, in view of the heavy rain, we had packed in a tin for safety. H. also carried almost our entire stock of cigarettes in the pocket of his shooting coat. Knowing his propensity for " falling in", I had some misgivings about this arrangement, but he insisted and I reluctantly agreed.

As we set off I reminded H. that some of the water holes in the immediate vicinity were quite deep. " Now for goodness sake be careful," I said, " and watch your step, you walk in front and I'll show you the way with the torch." " Not to worry," replied H., " I'll be careful." The words were hardly out of his mouth when, with a resounding splash, he stepped over the edge of a pool about a couple of feet deep, falling backwards into a sitting position against the bank. Cursing quietly and steadily, he rose to his feet, holding his gun in one hand and groping with his free hand for the game-bag which had slipped from his shoulder when he fell. Being well clad in oilskins and thigh-length boots, he was fortunately rather less wet than might have been expected, but he was by no means dry and the game-bag was a sodden mass. With the aid of the torch we inspected the contents; our packets of sandwiches were soaked and ruined but the cartridges appeared to be O.K. A horrible thought struck me, " The cigarettes ! What about the cigarettes? " H. unbuttoned his oilskin and put his hand into the pocket of his fowling coat. Carefully he withdrew a damp cardboard box. In the light of the torch it didn't look too good. Anxiously we opened the lid and peered in—our stock of cigarettes was destroyed. We looked at each other in dismay. The loss of the food was a nuisance, but the loss of the cigarettes was a real blow as we were both heavy smokers at that time. A hastily organised inventory revealed that we had exactly five dry cigarettes left between us.

Feeling none too happy we plodded on to the place where we had decided to await the geese. On arrival at our selected creek, I immediately slipped a couple of BBs into the chambers of my gun while H. was examining his to see if any mud or water had got into the barrels when he fell. Seconds later a goose called almost overhead. Looking up I caught a glimpse of a dark blob against the greying sky and a quick snap shot was followed by a hefty thump as a greylag hit the merse.

This cheered us up quite a lot and on the strength of this early success we smoked a couple of our slender stock of cigarettes. I had high hopes that from now on things were going to go well for us and that my friend would get his goose after all. But it was not to be. Shortly afterwards we heard geese approaching from the direction of the sands; it was still much too dark to see them, but they seemed to be heading straight for us. Suddenly, to our dismay, flashes of flame split the darkness ahead of us and a volley of shots rang out. We had been forestalled ! Unknown to us a party of four gunners had taken up position in the dark, right between us and the geese, the noise of the wind and rain drowning any sounds they might have made.

Although the geese came right on over our heads, by the time they reached us they had climbed up out of range and we never fired a shot. In the next half hour this happened twice more, the party ahead of us finishing the flight with a combined bag of nine geese while we looked on helplessly. Since there was no hope of recrossing the river at this state of the tide, we were compelled to wait for several hours, wet, hungry, and long since out of cigarettes. Eventually, when the tide turned, we packed up and, returning to the boat, rowed back across the river. On the way home we spotted a party of greylag feeding on the merse on our own side of the river and arranged to try for a shot at them the following morning if they returned to the same place.

Bright and early we took up our position, each in a different creek about 150 yards apart. The morning was much too calm for our liking, with a clear sky and a nip of frost, but since we hoped the geese would come in to land in the vicinity, we were not too discouraged by this. At first light we heard several lots of geese leave the sands and fly off westward, heading in almost the opposite direction to our position. This was discouraging to say the least, as we knew from experience that the first leavers usually set a pattern that the remainder of the geese would follow in due course. However, every wildfowler is a born optimist and we clung to the hope that the geese we had seen here yesterday would return, notwithstanding the general exodus.

As the light strengthened, skein after skein left the sands and all went off in the same direction. By the time it was full daylight the binoculars revealed only a little party of about 30 still left on the sands, and our chances of getting a shot appeared non-existent, yet against all reason we determined to hang on until the last little lot had gone. Having nothing better to do I watched them at frequent intervals through the binoculars and, finally, to the accompaniment of the usual goose " music " which carried clearly to us on the still air, they flapped along the sands and took off. As soon as they were all in the air the skein turned and headed in our direction and I knew these were our birds after all. Whistling to H. to make sure he knew they were coming, I watched the approach of the geese, and as they drew nearer I crouched in the bottom of the creek as close to the bank as I could get. In a surprisingly short time the sound of their voices rising in crescendo indicated that the " moment of truth " had almost come.

As usual my heart pounded with the terrific excitement that to me is inseparable from these occasions. I judged that the geese were somewhat to my right and turned in that direction. The next moment they crossed the creek in full view. They were a longish shot for me, but were heading straight for H. I kept as still as a statue. Seconds later two shots rang out in quick succession. I sprang erect in time to see a goose plummet into a nearby creek, and H., yelling in triumph, climb out of his hide and go rushing across to retrieve it. Shouting my congratulations, I also climbed out of my creek, taking my eye off H. for a moment or two while I did so. When I looked up again he was nowhere to be seen but almost at once he emerged from the creek into which the goose had dropped, and climbing over the edge walked across to meet me. I stopped in my tracks in utter astonishment: he was plastered with mud from head to foot. His eyes, through a mask of mud, sparkled with joy and in his right hand he held aloft a bundle of mud and feathers which was presumably his goose. The sight of him was more than I could stand and I burst into a fit of uncontrollable laughter.

When he reached me I shook his muddy hand, gasping out congratulations and questions between renewed bursts of laughter.

" Well done, old lad, but how on earth did you get in such a mess? "

" Well," he replied, " the goose dropped in a creek with about a foot of soft mud in the bottom, and I'm afraid I slipped getting over the bank, and fell on top of it." He grinned happily through the muck. A few minutes work in a nearby " puddle " wrought a transformation. The same treatment transformed his kill into a nice young grey-lag. We examined the goose with interest. It had taken a lot of getting, but we agreed it had been worth all the effort, and might well be the forerunner of many more.

PEREGRINES

S. Crook

Ferryman describes some experiences with these magnificent falcons

JIM HUMPHREY'S interesting account of the use of peregrines by the Royal Navy to counter the menace of birds on airfield runways (October 13, 1966) called to mind a number of incidents concerning these birds. I can well understand his conclusion that this is probably the most effective of bird-scaring devices as I have seen something of the terror they inspire among wildfowl and shore birds in general.

Only last winter a companion and I had a demonstration of how effectively peregrines can clear an area of foreshore of everything that flies. We were concealed among rocks on a foreshore much favoured by oyster-catchers, curlew and a variety of small waders, when suddenly masses of these and other birds came tearing along the shore at almost head height followed by a pair of peregrines. The falcons were no more than ten feet above the rocks and made no attempt to catch any of the panic-stricken waders, indeed we decided that they were not hunting at all, but probably on migration. Nevertheless their passing swept everything before them.

Although man may rightly regard himself as the most formidable enemy to wildfowl, it seems doubtful if the birds themselves so regard him. At any rate on more than one occasion hunted wildfowl have almost completely ignored my presence in their frantic efforts to escape the fleet winged terror that pursued them. An outstanding example of this occurred in the winter of 1949-50. I was lying in my punt watching a number of wigeon swimming about amongst ice floes in the river. The punt, camouflaged with snow, was lying near the edge of a large tidal pool, the surface of which was almost entirely covered by an inch or two of slush ice, and I was waiting in the hope of the wigeon becoming sufficiently concentrated to offer the chance of a puntgun shot. Although I did not know it I was not the only hunter interested in those wigeon.

After a time three of them took off and flew down river towards me at a height of about 20 feet. When they were almost abreast of the punt I was astonished to see them suddenly stop flying and drop like stones into the pool, striking the slush ice with such force that they went straight through and vanished instantly. At almost the same moment a peregrine, the wind whistling through its pinions, struck the ice at the same spot and, ricocheting into the air, shot up to a great height in a twinkling and disappeared from my sight. With keen interest I looked towards the spot where the wigeon had vanished. After a considerable lapse of time three little heads appeared at the surface and, since they were quite close by, I could plainly see their eyes fearfully searching the sky for their terrible enemy. Whether or not they could still see the falcon I do not know, but after a brief interval they quietly submerged, and for the next ten minutes or so this procedure was repeated time and again. That they were well aware of my presence there is not the slightest doubt, as I could see them looking towards me from time to time; but not until they were satisfied that the peregrine was no longer hanging about did they fully emerge from the icy water and, after floating on the surface for a time, while we literally stared each other in the face, finally took off and, flying back up river, rejoined the main body.

On another occasion my nephew and I witnessed a peregrine successfully attacking a company of pintail. When we first sighted them the pintail were flying at a terrific pace a few feet above the water, the falcon keeping station above and behind them. The duck were keeping such close formation that an almost continuous cracking sound was audible as the wing-tips overlapped and collided. Suddenly the peregrine shot ahead and the pintail instantly turned and flew in the opposite direction. During the operation one unfortunate drake, possibly a pricked bird, lost his place in the formation and was immediately cut out by the falcon and given no chance of rejoining the ranks. Side-slipping to avoid the falcon's stoop, the drake made off at a tangent across the merse on the opposite side of the river from our viewpoint, hotly pursued by the falcon which again stooped from a considerable height. Once again the pintail succeeded in avoiding the swoop, but this time the peregrine, taking advantage of the speed of its dive, came whistling up from below and, turning on its back at the last moment, seized the pintail with its talons. The two birds, locked together in a melee of thrashing wings, fluttered to the ground where the grim struggle continued for a long time, the falcon apparently having considerable difficulty in killing the drake.

This method of taking prey is, I believe, known as " binding on," and this was the only time I saw a bird taken in this fashion. The usual method employed by the peregrine is to strike the prey with the talons at the end of a terrific " power-dive " and this almost always results in the prey being killed or maimed. Quite recently my son and I witnessed a peregrine terrorising a company of wigeon. We were concealed on the river-bank and saw the wigeon approach up-river, flying in close formation at a tremendous speed a few feet above the water. I have never seen wigeon flying faster. Like the pintail previously mentioned, they were so densely packed that their wings continually cracked together, while their thrashing pinions created a high-pitched whistling sound that could be heard a long way off. Above and behind came the peregrine, for all the world like a collie herding sheep. Every now and then, apparently without effort, the falcon would shoot ahead of the wigeon, which would instantly turn and go tearing off in the opposite direction, only to be turned again at any moment the peregrine chose.

There is little doubt that the close formation and low altitude adopted by these duck was the best possible method of protection against attack, as it is extremely unlikely that any predator would risk damage to its wings by attacking such a dense mass of birds. The moment of peril obviously comes if the company panics and breaks up, or if an individual loses its place in the formation, as in the case of the pintail.

Although it kills almost all its prey, I know of at least one instance where a peregrine was apparently prepared to take a bird already dead. A friend of mine, while concealed in a stone hide, shot a wigeon which fell dead on the sands close by. Since the bird was lying in full view, my friend, who did not have a dog with him, did not bother to pick it up at the time. Some time later a peregrine appeared on the scene and pitched on the sand beside the wigeon. Unfortunately it spotted my friend almost at once and cleared off, so we do not know whether it would have eaten the wigeon on the spot or have attempted to carry it off, although I think the former is much more likely.

MOONLIGHT FORAY

remembered by Ferryman

I gaped at the birds in shocked astonishment . . . .

Noel Dudley

IT was one of those rare mornings that gladden a puntsman's heart. The waning moon shone softly through a thin layer of cloud, while a light breeze ruffled the water darkening the surface mirror that otherwise might have shown up a punt to watchful fowl.

And so it was that as I made my way down the creek-side to where the punt lay anchored, my step was light despite the heavy load of gear I carried. Dawn was still almost three hours away and it was my intention to row down the estuary for a distance of several miles and there await the arrival of the duck from their feeding grounds, this method of attack having proved by far the most successful. Dumping my load of gear on the grass I was just about to remove the cover from the punt when I heard a goose call. This was quickly answered by another and a short altercation took place, then once again the morning was quiet except for the sigh of the wind and the sound of the tide pouring through the salmon net stakes.

But my plans were instantly changed: here was a chance not to be missed—there were geese in the Gut and the fever burned in me like a bright flame. The Gut was one of the few places where it was possible to attack the geese with the punt, but it was not one of their normal roosting grounds, and was only visited occasionally, usually by small parties, when the moon was waning or " sitting," as we called it. Quietly and with an efficiency born from long practise I whipped the cover off the punt and loaded the big muzzle-loading punt-gun, ramming down the powder and topping it with the 19 ounces of BB shot she fired. at the same time listening intently for any sound from the geese in order to gauge their position as near as possible.

The Gut, a subsidiary channel of the tidal river, lay at no great distance from our mooring creek, and presently, everything ready for .action, I slipped down the creek, pushing the punt along with a setting-pole tipped with lead, designed to make the minimum of sound on the somewhat gravelly bottom. Arriving at the junction of the creek and the main river, I lay-to for a time listening carefully, and finally, deciding that the geese must be sitting on the right-hand edge of the Gut, I lay down and commenced setting the punt upstream against the considerable ebb tide still running. When I had covered about half the estimated distance I got out the binoculars and took a look ahead. Since their initial outburst the geese had made hardly any sound; doubtless many of them would be asleep and only an occasional low pitched sound came from them. It is always difficult to see sitting birds in dim moonlight, and at first I could distinguish nothing, particularly since I was looking into the gloom of the river's high banks, and then I thought I could just make out a line of black blobs along the channel's edge where the wavelets were faintly tinged with moonlight. That must be the geese!

As always, I felt a tremendous surge of excitement and my heart pounded like mad. With infinite care I put down the binoculars and, taking the setting-pole in my right hand, pushed on upstream as quietly as possible. Slowly but surely the punt forged ahead, her bow sliding through the water with only a faint hiss and a gentle tap, tap of the wavelets. My excitement mounted as the minutes passed. I knew I must be getting close, that at any moment now I ought to see them, and that once I was able to do so in this light they would be within range and I could shoot at will. I cocked the action of the gun. With my left hand resting on the gunstock, ready to swing it if necessary, I eased the punt forward yard by yard.

The geese were now completely silent, not a whisper of sound was to be heard. Anxiously I stared ahead, fearful that they had sensed my approach and would jump before I could see them properly. And then there they were . . . ! A dark line of birds swimming out from a little bay where the channel curved outwards. They were well within range and had been almost invisible until they had moved out into the channel. I sighted along the gun barrel: it was bearing right down their line and needed no correction. With the setting-pole I rapped smartly on the side of the punt, seized the lanyard and pulled! A tongue of flame leapt from the gun muzzle, the boom of the shot rolled like thunder in the nearby hills and a pandemonium of sound shattered the quiet of the morning. With a tremendous clamour the geese took off. For a moment I could see nothing through the pall of gunsmoke, but the noise of the geese left no doubt that a very large number of birds had been present. Dropping the grapnel over the stern, I grabbed the cripple-stopper and cartridge bag and, stepping over the side of the punt into the water, waded ashore. Dashing forward, clear of the thinning smoke, I looked to see the results of my shot . . . A bullseye . . . !

The water ahead was dotted with the dark outline of floating birds, among which were several swimmers. These I dispatched with the cripple-stopper, missing once or twice in the tricky light which was getting dimmer all the time as the moon sank towards the horizon. Some distance ahead I could hear a goose calling and flapping on the water. Wading ahead through the shallows I killed it with one shot as it flapped along the surface.

Satisfied that all the cripples had now been dealt with I hurried back to the punt to commence the pick-up. The birds were drifting downstream fairly quickly and I did not want any of them to get below my position. Quickly the grapnel was hauled up, the punt's head turned upstream, and facing forward in a kneeling position I commenced to paddle. A few strokes sufficed to take me to the nearest bird. It looked very dark for a goose and rather small. I felt vaguely uneasy. Reaching over the side I scooped it up and my heart sank . . . a wigeon . . .! I gaped at it in shocked astonishment. Hastily I paddled to the next bird . . . another wigeon . . . and another . . . and another . . . I was shattered. I had never even suspected the presence of wigeon, and yet I had fired at a company that must have been sitting just downstream from the geese. Then I remembered the last cripple I had shot—that had been a goose without any doubt. There must be geese among them!

Paddling from bird to bird as they drifted down to me I counted 19 . . . 20 . . . 21 . . . 22 wigeon. Beyond I could see only one other bird on the water. I picked up the glasses. Yes! That looked like a goose all right. That would be the cripple I had shot. Oh well, one goose anyway. But what was that lying on the mud a few yards back from the water's edge? And beyond? These were no wigeon . . . My spirits rose. I had hit some of the geese after all. Picking up the paddle I retrieved the floating bird and shot the punt ashore. Two greylags lay within a yard of each other. Beyond I could see several other objects on the mud that could be other geese. They were. I picked up four more greylags, making a total of seven.

The geese had evidently remained on the mud when the wigeon swam out and only the fact that the shoreline curved round to the left resulted in any of the pattern having struck the geese, and that only at extreme range. As there was a good chance of finding a dropper or two on the mud, I determined to stay in the area of the shot until daylight.

The author after a successful shot on another occasion.

Stowing the birds and cleaning and reloading the gun helped to pass the time away, and as soon as there was sufficient light I began a systematic search of the mud and creeks, etc., on each side of the river for at least a quarter-of-a-mile above and below the scene of the shot. This resulted in my picking up five more wigeon, one of which was partly eaten by great black-backed gulls. and two more geese, thus bringing the total for the shot to 27 wigeon and 9 geese. There is little doubt that had the wigeon not intervened I would have shot a good many more geese, but even so I was very happy. It wasn't every day one bagged both wigeon and geese with the one shot.

A Shot in the Dark

Ferryman describes an early episode with a 4-bore

...but the terriffic recoil knocked me backwards.....   Noel Dudley

WHEN the Major first appeared in our village with the 4-bore, I was still only an early teenager. Not that the term was ever applied to us in those days. There were other terms, usually designed to impress on us the fact that we were very small fry indeed. Nevertheless, as soon as I saw it I wanted that great gun for myself. A single-barrel underlever breech loader, with an enormously strong breech, it looked capable of bringing down an aircraft. How I longed to lay hands on that mighty weapon. . .

Young as I was I had known the Major for some time, having haunted his winter headquarters in the "Fish House" for years. I had even enjoyed the unforgettable privilege and thrill of having been out with him in his double punt on a number of occasions, and had had the benefit of his expert tuition in this branch of the sport. In those days the Major, together with his right-hand man Adam, were the leading lights among puntsmen in our part of the country. The standards they set, both in gear and technique, were the ones others aspired to.

One day, noting my interest in the 4-bore, the Major invited me to examine the gun. It was so heavy I could hardly get it to my shoulder and could only hold it there when the barrel was pointing upwards at a fairly acute angle so that my shoulder supported most of the weight. I remarked that it ought to bring down a goose from a considerable height, whereupon to my surprise and delight the Major offered to lend it to me on a day of my own choosing. It was then and there arranged that I should borrow the gun for a foray against the geese on the following Saturday. On the Friday night I went along to the "Fish House" to collect the 4-bore so that I could get off as quickly as possible after lunch the following day. I should have liked to have been out for morning flight, but having to work until noon on Saturday made this impossible. Nevertheless, I felt quite hopeful of getting a shot as the geese were feeding on the merse almost every day and, having been moved off, would frequently return again within an hour or two. Handing over the gun and four cartridges loaded with BiB, the Major wished me luck, but warned that I must on no account fire the gun from the top of my shoulder, as this might result in a broken collar bone.

Next day, having crossed the river in the little black punt known as the "Coffin," I stood facing seaward on the sloping side of a deep and wide creek. All around me the merse was speckled with goose droppings and, indeed, my arrival had put a party of greylags off this very area. The 4-bore, loaded and ready, lay on the grass in front of me, and every now and then I picked it up and hoisting its massive weight to my shoulder, took a practise swing. Some time later I was joined by a fowler of great experience (later to become a fast and lifelong friend) of whom I had heard, but never previously met. He was suitably impressed by the 4-bore, and remained to chat for a while. He was just about to leave when we heard geese approaching, whereupon he immediately took cover in my creek, and soon we could see a large skein heading in our direction. As they drew nearer he remarked that they were too high for his 12-bore, "but you ought," quoth he, "to be able to knock one down with that cannon." Cocking the massive hammer on the side of the gun, I knelt on the sloping mud, and with the barrel resting on the edge of the bank, awaited with pounding heart

26

and some anxiety, the oncoming geese. In a clamour of sound they swept into view. With a mighty effort I hoisted the 4-bore to my shoulder, pointed the gun about halfway along one leg of the skein, and remembering the Major's warning, leaned well back and pulled the trigger. Whether or not my insecure stance contributed to my downfall I do not know, but the terrific recoil knocked me backwards, head over heels, and the next moment I found myself lying on the soft mud of the creek bottom with the 4-bore on top of me. My friend, having assured himself that I, like the geese, was unhurt, had a hearty laugh at my expense and shortly afterwards went off with his spaniel at his heels, leaving behind a very chastened young man.

The afternoon wore on and darkness began to fall without my having had another chance to try out the big gun. In the gloaming great herds of curlew flighted down the estuary to roost on the sands, interspersed with rafts of gulls. I hardly gave them a second glance. As it grew dark the wigeon began to flight, and several times I might have had a good chance if I had been armed with a lighter weapon, but I had eyes and ears only for the geese, and so far only distant voices told me of several skeins coming in from the westward to roost on the sands. Soon it got too dark to see the flighting wigeon except against one small area of afterglow. Apart from this area the sky was now velvety black and bright with stars—it was time to go home. Shouldering the 4-bore, I made my way back to the river bank, the lights from the village opposite acting as a sure guide. Laying the gun down on the grass, I was groping among the seaweed-covered stones for the punt's anchor when I heard geese approaching down-river. Hastily picking up the gun I listened intently. Yes. . . ! They were coming straight down-river towards me, and judging from the sound were flying at no great height. Slipping a cartridge into the breech I looked upwards. There was little hope of seeing them, but—well, you never know—I cocked the hammer. Sitting facing the oncoming geese, my legs over the edge of a cut brew, I strained my eyes into the darkness. Soon they were almost overhead, and I could hear not only their voices, but the sound of their wings as well, but still not a thing could I see. Almost in despair I stared upwards and as the geese swept over and beyond me I clewed round and, without conscious thought, pointed the gun at the sound and pulled the trigger. A great tongue of flame leapt from the gun-muzzle blinding me for the moment and then to my unspeakable joy two hefty thumps in quick succession proclaimed the success of my shot in the dark.

Behind the sea-wall protecting the river bank ran a wide creek, its bottom consisting of deep, soft mud, and into this both geese had fallen. This would have been no great problem if I had remembered to bring a flashlight, but I had nothing but a few matches, and these were quickly expended during which time I had found only one goose half buried in the mud and only saved from complete immersion because its wings were outspread. After groping about in the dark for some time I gave up the attempt and decided to come back again in the morning to search for the remaining goose, not that I shad much hope of finding it after the tide had been over the mud, but there was always a chance.

The following day being Sunday I had plenty of time in which to search, but as soon as it was clear enough to see properly I rowed across in the "Coffin" and after anchoring the punt, walked over to the big creek. At first glance the sides and bottom looked smooth and bare, and then I spotted something sticking up out of the mud. Quickly I reached the spot—it was the tip of a wing showing above the mud—and I knew at once I had found my other goose. I hauled it out and carrying it over to a nearby water-hole, washed off the mud and found it soaked but otherwise none the worse. And so home in triumph with a fine tale to tell my friend the Major when I returned his gun carefully cleaned and oiled, and the remaining two cartridges.

It was not until some time afterwards that it occurred to me that my second shot had neither knocked me over nor inconvenienced me in any way, and for some reason I was mildly surprised.

DARK STALK
by Ferryman

...impatiently I waited for the geese to call again.

Noel Dudley

It was one of those nights when the entire world seemed locked in the iron grip of King Frost. The young moon had already set, but the sky was ablaze with stars and their cold light, reflected from the powdering of snow that lay on the ground, gave the night a surprising luminosity. As I stood looking across the river, smoking a final cigarette, and admiring the beauty of the night, I was struck by the almost complete silence, broken only as a wader moved from its roost on the sands by the slowly flowing tide, called plaintively.

Flicking away my cigarette end, I turned homeward, the thought of my warm bed waiting only a couple of hundred yards away was very pleasant. Suddenly I stopped in my tracks—a goose had called from the merse edge less than half-a-mile from where I stood! Motionless I waited for another call; it was a long time coming, and the piercing cold was beginning to chill me to the bone. Then once again it came—the call of a greylag—quietly, only just audible and, as near as I could judge, from exactly the same place ! Cold, bed, everything else was forgotten. Once again goose fever had me in its grip—here was a chance not to be missed.

Occasionally small parties of geese roosted on the mudbanks close to the merse edge at this point, and on nights such as this it was sometimes possible to stalk them down one of the numerous creeks that drained the merse, always providing one knew exactly where they were. In little more than half-an-hour I crouched in a creek a few hundred yards from where I estimated the goose had called. Before I could move any closer I had to be certain I was in the right creek and only another call could tell me that. As a result of my hurried preparations and rapid walk across the frozen merse I was, to begin with, comfortably warm, but soon the intense cold began to penetrate even through my warm fowling gear and I hoped the geese would not be too long in announcing their whereabouts. Almost an hour dragged past without a single sound from them. By now I was feeling the cold acutely, and my feet felt as though they were no longer part of my body. I peered at my watch—ten minutes to midnight—I would wait until midnight and not a moment longer. If by then I had heard nothing I felt it would be fairly safe to assume that the geese had moved on before I arrived on the scene.

On the stroke of midnight (I could hear it chiming on the village clock) I climbed stiffly out of my creek and with some reluctance set out for home. Before I had taken 50 paces a goose called and was answered by another, then once again silence settled over the frozen merseland. But I now knew all I needed to know—the geese were still there and I had not been in the right creek. Hastily retracing my steps I carried on up the merse until I reached a creek which I knew from experience would bring me to the mud at a point very close to where I had heard the geese call. The tide was now on the ebb and since it had not even reached the point at which I entered the creek, I anticipated little difficulty with this. There was, however, another and serious difficulty. The creek bottom was covered by a sheet of thin ice overlying the mud and this sometimes broke when trodden on, so that every step had to be made with the utmost care to avoid making any noise. As a result of this, progress was very slow, but eventually I reached a part of the creek from which the tide had not yet ebbed and progress became easier, for although the bottom was still ice covered, the overlying water muffled the sound of the breaking ice.

The closer I got to the mouth of the creek the deeper the water became, and as I rounded the final bend I was compelled to abandon the creek-bottom and slither along the icy slope above the water line. This was very hard going and instead of being half frozen I was now perspiring like mad. Having got as far down the creek as I possibly could, I loaded the gun and was in the act of crawling up the icy slope when I dislodged a sheet of ice which slid tinkling down into the water below, making a noise that set my taut nerves on edge. A moment later a goose called so close by it startled me, low pitched but insistent—an alarm call ! Frantically, my heart thumping with excitement, I scrabbled up the icy slope and peered over the top. About 15 yards away, dimly silhouetted against the starlit shimmer of the water, a line of dark forms was moving down the mudbank. They reached the water's edge and launched themselves into the tide as I cocked the hammers of my gun. Pointing at the dark mass I fired both barrels in rapid succession. With a great outcry and thrashing of wings the geese took off.

Reloading as I went I ran down to the tide's edge—four dark forms lay on the water, but no *coup-de-grace* was necessary—they were all dead. Delighted at the success of my stalk I waded carefully towards the nearest bird. There was need for care as the mudbank at this point was very steep and extremely slippery, the ice which had formed between the tides having remained unthawed even though covered by the tide. I was somewhat disconcerted to discover that by the time I reached the bird the water was almost up to the top of my waders. Tossing the goose ashore I carefully edged my way towards the next bird. When I thought I was close enough I reached out with the barrels of my gun towards the floating goose. I was an inch or two short—just one more step and I had him ! At that precise moment both feet shot from under me and the icy water closed over my head. The shock was so great that I opened my mouth in an involuntary gasp, and immediately had it filled with muddy water. Choking and gasping I struggled to my feet; I had slid so far forward that I was now chest deep in the water, but I was still in possession of my gun. There were now two geese within easy reach and these I quickly grabbed and towed ashore. The remaining goose had drifted a little way downstream but there was now no problem about securing it. I simply waded out as far as was necessary without worrying too much about the depth. It was just as well. The excitement of the pick-up now being over I began to feel the effects of my soaked clothing and realised I would have to get home as quickly as possible.

Returning with my kill to the merse edge I sat down on the frozen grass, peeled off my sea-boots and socks, removed as much water as possible and replaced both. Tying the necks of the geese together I slung them over my shoulder, and picking up my gun set out at a jog-trot for home. Running and walking alternately I reached home in a comparatively short time, but so bitter was the cold that my clothing was encased with ice and my trousers so stiff that I was obliged to thaw them out in front of the stove before I could get them off. I must have looked extremely odd as my father, the most phlegmatic of men, remarked upon seeing me that " it must be freezing very hard " which was about the only comment he ever made concerning my appearance after a wildfowling expedition.

It only remains to record that after a hot bath and a " nice cup of tea " I was nothing the worse for my midnight dip, but although I enjoyed the stalk very much I cannot honestly say I enjoyed *that* part of it.

BIG SHOT

Ferryman remembers the chance of a lifetime

BECAUSE low water did not occur until the middle of the forenoon, it was broad daylight by the time the little single punt lay-to off the mouth of the tributary. The leaden sky held the threat of rain, while a fresh south-westerly wind kicked up a nasty " jabble " that made punting difficult, but was just the thing to make the duck sit tight.

The glasses revealed that the little river held a fair number of duck, mainly pintail, with a few shoveler and a sprinkling of wigeon, but nothing like the number I had expected to find there. The nearest pintail, about 60 in number, were clustered thickly on a mud point formed by a bend in the tributary, and looked a fair chance. However, before committing myself to an attempt on them, I decided to risk a quick look down the main river, even though this meant standing up in the punt and possibly alarming the duck in the tributary. Almost at once a dark patch caught my eye, and focusing the glasses I saw at once that it consisted of an enormous company of wigeon packed so closely together as to form an apparently solid mass.

The pintail were immediately forgotten—come what may, I would have to try for a shot at this mighty company, even though at first sight the chance of success did not appear to be very bright. The wigeon were sitting on the mud alongside the dried-out bed of the old west channel. No doubt they had pitched there when the channel still held water, but now the tide had ebbed away and the nearest water that would float the punt was at least half a mile to seaward. To reach this it would be necessary to push down the main channel for more than a mile in order to outflank the sand-cum-mudbank separating the two channels, and having done so, to await the flood tide to float the punt up to the wigeon. The only alternative I could think of was to put the wigeon up and hope they would pitch in the main channel where I could attack them without delay. I was none too keen to be far down the bay when the flood tide came as I expected the wind to freshen, and the water was certain to become very rough as soon as the outer sandbanks covered. With the aid of the binoculars I took another look at the duck ; they appeared to be almost asleep and were a sight to drive caution to the four winds. I decided to attack them on the flood!

As I had to pass within a couple of hundred yards of the wigeon en route, it was necessary to drop down river in the prone position. This presented little difficulty as there was ample time and the swift current swept the punt along in good style. When the punt, almost wholly concealed by the intervening mudbank, came opposite the wigeon, I took a peep at them over the edge of the coaming. The sight made me catch my breath! I hesitate to estimate how many birds were in that vast company, but there must have been many thousands. Not a head was up, and the entire multitude appeared to be sound asleep. Quietly I pushed on past, and eventually, on reaching a narrow gut through which the water rushed into the west channel, shot the punt through. A long wait followed, but at last the tide turned and as soon as the first signs of the flood became apparent I set off slowly up the channel.

A long way ahead of me I could see, even with the naked eye, the great dark patch that was the wigeon. Slowly the tide began to gather momentum and gradually I increased my rate of progress. My aim was, if possible, to arrive in range at the precise moment the water had reached sufficient depth. To arrive too soon would have invited disaster, as the punt on taking the ground would almost certainly have broached to and I might not have been able to control it. To arrive late would be equally disastrous, as I expected the wigeon to move the moment the tide reached them. Pushing along quietly with my shortest pole, I gradually closed the gap between the punt and the still dry part of the channel ahead. The tide was now moving up it quite briskly, thrusting ahead of it a little foam-crested bore an inch or two high. On reaching the minimum depth in which the punt would safely float, I adjusted its speed to match that of the tide.

Minute after minute fled past and nearer and nearer I drew to that mighty company. The punt was now moving along at a brisk pace, and a venture that had begun as a somewhat forlorn hope now took on a very different appearance. I stole one last look at the wigeon ; they were little more than 400 yards away ; my heart beat faster and a tremendous excitement gripped me. Reaching over the edge of the coaming I made a final adjustment to the elevation of the gun, cocked the firing mechanism and laid the lanyard in a handy position. Everything was now ready for action! A minute passed—another ; through the space between the gun and the coaming my eyes were fixed on the little tidal bore as it advanced steadily up the channel-bed ; only in this way could I be sure of keeping the punt in the correct position. Suddenly a dark mass swam into view to my right front—the wigeon—I was almost up to them! My right leg started to tremble uncontrollably.

Steadily the distance shortened, 150, 120 —100 yards! Slowly I counted up to ten and then with all my power I shot the punt forward, at the same time pushing the stern to port in order to get the gun to bear. With my left hand on the gun-stock I raised my head—the sight that greeted me was almost beyond belief! The mudbank ahead was a solid mass of duck stretching away in a great oval formation. Already I was within long range—another second or two and it wouldn't matter if they jumped—I would shoot flying. Rapidly the range shortened—Now ... ! At that moment the tide reached the nearest of the wigeon and on that instant their heads shot up. Letting go the setting-pole I seized the lanyard and swinging the muzzle of the gun as far as possible to the right in order to shoot obliquely across the width of the company, instead of right up through their ranks, I gave it a firm pull.

With a great boom the gun went off and 19 ounces of B.B. sped on its way! At almost the same instant the punt took the ground. Through the thinning smoke I could see that the results of the shot were all that I expected —the mud bank was strewn with dead and crippled duck. Tossing the grapnel over the side I grabbed my 12-bore and cartridge bag and waded off toward the nearest group of cripples. To my dismay I found the mud much softer than I had expected, but I ploughed on through it as best I could and working round from right to left dealt with the considerable, number of cripples. By the time they were all accounted for I was a long way from the punt, and since the tide was now covering the mud banks very quickly indeed I was forced to rush back to the punt before the water became too deep to wade. By the time I reached it I was so exhausted that I was compelled to lie in the cockpit and rest before I could do any more. Ahead of me I could see the results of my shot scatter far and wide as the tide floated them off the mud. I groaned in dismay—my biggest shot ever and I hadn't even a single duck in the punt! Summoning the necessary energy from somewhere, I set off in pursuit of the floating duck. Working like a trojan I eventually picked up all except about a dozen of them. These had floated over the mudbank into the main channel and I was forced to leave them for the time being.

The wind, as had been foreseen, was now blowing very strongly, a nasty chop was rapidly building up and the heavily laden punt was shipping a lot of water. With the long setting pole I worked the punt obliquely across the mudbank, the quartering waves continuing to break over the coaming during the process. In the main channel a big sea was running so, before venturing out in search of the remaining wigeon, I bailed as much water as possible out of the punt, meantime holding her head on to the sea with my free hand. A hasty look through the glasses revealed no sign of the duck which I knew must have drifted a long way ahead, so kneeling in the only little space available in the stern. I seized the paddle and set off in pursuit.

With the wind and tide behind me I made fair progress, but the sea was now alarmingly rough, and only the fact that I was running before it made it possible to continue. Even so the punt shipped a lot of water which I was unable to do anything about it, as I was fully occupied in keeping her on a straight course. Above the mouth of the tributary the river narrowed considerably and the sea was much less rough ; and there I saw it, the first of my lost duck. Shortly afterwards I spotted three others and eventually all four were retrieved. Since I could see no sign of the remainder I decided to cross the river and in the shelter of the old quay to bail the punt and get things a little more shipshape. On arrival, I threw out all the duck, bailed the punt dry and reloaded the duck, counting them as I did so. I had picked up 64 wigeon. It only remains to record that seven others were recovered along the tide's edge by acquaintances, making a total of 71 known to have been picked up.

BONUS GEESE

Noel Dudley

Ferryman recalls occasions when the unexpected has prevailed

FOR a goose addict, I suppose one of the great advantages of actually living in goose country is the fact that no matter what one sets out to shoot, there is always the chance, however slim, of returning with a bonus of one or more of these fowl in the bag. In fact, in looking back over the years I find that this has happened on a surprising number of occasions, even when conditions were such that the chances of shooting one by orthodox methods were almost hopeless. Very occasionally these bonus geese have been obtained with ridiculous ease, having by the merest chance happened along and flown within range.

More often they have had to be worked for, and sometimes worked for very strenuously indeed ! As an example of the first category I recall a warm sunny afternoon in late October, when scarcely a breath of wind stirred the long merse grass and as I sat basking in the sun on an upturned oil-drum in a creek, I was more than half asleep. The purpose of my visit was to try for a shot or two at some of the golden plover I had spotted here the previous afternoon. So far they had failed to turn up, but what of it, it was a pleasant day to be out. Lulled by the hum of insects, I drowsed comfortably on my oil-drum. A single thrilling call pierced the mists of sleep and instantly I was awake. Geese . . . and close . . ! Over the grassy fringe of the creek I peered in frank disbelief—a pair of greylag were flying straight at me. No time to change the No. 5 shot cartridges for the pair of BB's I always carried for just such an opportunity, time enough only to cock the hammers of my gun. A moment or two later the geese were almost straight overhead. It was the easiest of shots and my right and left had them " dead in the air." They dropped on the clean merse grass almost unmarked, and I could scarcely believe my good fortune.

About half-an-hour later, having, in the meantime, bagged five golden plover from a party that whizzed past shortly after I had retrieved the geese, I spotted five birds in the distance. They were approaching almost out of the eye of the sun and were difficult to see clearly, but they had the look of geese and if they kept on coming there was a good chance that they would pass within range of me. I thought eagerly, " my goodness wouldn't it be great if they did turn out to be geese ! " Through half shut eyelids I squinted at them as they approached through the shimmering haze. Then came the distant call that set all doubts at rest.—" They were greylag after all!" Quickly changing the cartridges I watched and waited ; they came straight at me, higher than the first pair, but well within range. When they were directly overhead I stood up and my rapid right and left brought two more greylag crashing to the merse.

On another occasion I was shooting pigeon in a rape field when a skein of about 50 greylag appeared on the scene, and after flying around for a time eventually pitched in a field about half-a-mile away on the other side of the river. Within a few minutes they had been put up by shots fired by another shooter and headed my way. Slipping my "emergency " BBs into my gun, I watched them without any real hope. Nonetheless they flew slap over my hide, and although they were rather high—indeed I was in two minds whether or not to fire—I managed by holding well ahead to knock down two of them, both of which were shot, rather luckily, through the head. Into the second category fall two events, remarkable chiefly because of the success that attended them, for they were the father and mother of forlorn hopes. My quarry on the first occasion was again golden plover, many hundreds of which were frequenting a number of flat marshy fields by the side of our tidal river. When moving from field to field parties of these birds often zoomed just over the tops of the high hedges which were a feature of the place at that time. I was concealed in a ditch at a gap in one such hedge, waiting for the plover flocks as they flashed over, when about 20 greylag came gaggling along and pitched in the middle of a nearby field. As usual my attention was focussed on the geese and I racked my brains for a plan by which I might conceivably get a shot at them.

The situation looked completely hopeless, the geese were right in the middle of the field which was very large and almost as flat as a board. There was not a vestage of cover except a few clumps of thistles, but grazing in the field was a large flock of sheep. Sheep. . . Now there was an idea ! How like a sheep did one have to look to remain unnoticed in the flock ? Could it be done ? The more I thought of it the more convinced I became that it was at least worth a try. Through the glasses I could see that some of the sheep were grazing very close to the geese without causing the least sign of alarm. I also noted that little groups of sheep were scattered across the field right up to the hedge and ditch by which I would have to approach. I decided to have a go !

Under my duffle coat I was wearing a large off-white jersey, so large indeed that a facetious member of the family had dubbed it my " maternity jersey " ! With this pulled well down over my bottom I thought I might stand a chance of remaining unnoticed by the geese. To conceal my face I decided to pull the roll collar of the jersey right over the top of my head, leaving only a small peep-hole in front of my eyes. Leaving my coat and other gear behind I set off up the ditch, carrying only my gun and a couple of spare cartridges. Having got into position, I crawled over the edge of the ditch, keeping the thickest bunch of sheep between myself and the geese. Worming along on my stomach I made quite good progress and covered the first half of the distance without incident. Pausing for a breather behind a convenient clump of thistles, I had a look to see how the geese were reacting ; they were grazing among the sheep and taking no notice of me whatsoever !

Again I set off keeping as close to the ground as possible and sliding the gun through the grass with my right hand. A little bunch of sheep were giving me wonderful cover, and I discovered that if I moved slowly enough I could keep them drifting ahead of me in exactly the right direction. On the other hand if I got too near they became distinctly uneasy and showed a tendency to bolt, and I had to be very careful not to press them too closely. Slowly I drew nearer where I estimated the geese to be. From my prone position they were extremely difficult to see, but eventually I spotted one through a little gap among the sheep. It was standing very much on the alert, and although the range was rather long I decided not to attempt to crawl any closer. Carefully drawing my knees up under me I cocked the hammers of my gun, sprang erect and dashed at top speed towards the goose I had marked down. I must have caught them completely unawares, because I covered quite a bit of ground before they were up and away. Sliding to a stop I let fly at the goose from which I had never taken my eyes. To my dismay my first shot had no apparent effect, but fortunately my second connected and the goose flopped to the ground as my four legged allies fled in every direction ! It was a splendid greylag and weighed 10½lb.

Profiting from the foregoing experience, I subsequently successfully stalked a small party of pinkfeet under even more unlikely circumstances. Following a morning's punting, my son and I were waiting until the tide reached sufficient depth to float the punt up to our moorings when seven pinkfeet pitched on the merse about 200 yards away. Since it was impossible to stalk them under cover, it was decided that I would attempt another " sheep crawl." All around us the merse was dotted with grazing sheep although none were in our immediate vicinity. We decided, therefore, to attempt to deceive the geese into believing that I actually was a sheep. I was wearing a well-worn and stained off-white duffle coat which was about the right colour. I then put my grey balaclava on back to front, allowing it to hang down in front of my face like a kind of snout and crawled over the edge of the creek on my hands and knees. The geese instantly stood on the alert, but I remained motionless and after a time some of them lowered their heads and commenced feeding. Lowering my own head I went through the motions of grazing and then very slowly commenced to crawl through the rough grass towards the geese.

Through my peepholes I watched them covertly and whenever they all stopped feeding and looked in my direction I at once halted and proceeded with my " grazing." Each time this happened I expected the geese to be up and away, but after watching for a time they always relaxed and resumed feeding, not even walking away from me !

Very, very slowly I drew nearer and I believe I could have crawled to close range had not a long and deep water-hole intervened right across my path. This completely stuck me. I could not crawl through it and I could not outflank it, as this would mean turning side oil to the geese, and they would never have stood for that ! There was only one thing for it—to get as close as possible and fire from there. Crawling right up to the edge of the water I yanked off the balaclava, straightened up and fired at the nearest goose at it rose into the air. The heavy charge from the 3 inch struck home, but the goose carried on and it took another shot to bring it down—a well earned bonus goose if ever there was one !

The Pukka Sahib

A curlew flight remembered by Ferryman

HAVING recently been looking back over close on half a century's wildfowling, the fact has become abundantly clear that although I have spent countless enjoyable and satisfying hours alone, the most pleasurable memories by far are of occasions when this enjoyment has been shared by others. Even in retrospect the incidents, and more particularly the people associated with them, have lost little of their interest and charm.

Perhaps I have been luckier than most, but I can think of no companion with whom I have shot, whose company I did not enjoy, or whose pleasure I did, not fully share, and though all too many are no longer with us, the memory of them is still heart-warming.

A right and left

People like my dear friend Hugh, companion on so many enjoyable and exciting adventures, who gave his valiant young life on the beaches of Normandy; of my friend Bob who was always going to give up wildfowling, but never did until death claimed him also; of Angus who pulled me out of the quicksand; of the Major whose grounding in the art of punting has stood me in good stead all these years; of Adam whose help and kindness in my boyhood I remember with gratitude; of my brother Jack, companion in a thousand; of many, many others who march through my thoughts like an army of friendly ghosts, calling up memories of days gone by. The Pukka Sahib ! Somehow I always think of him by this term. He had been a Major in the Indian army and had, he assured me, hunted tiger in the jungle, shot duck by the cartload in the *jheels*, chikhor and sisi in the foothills, peafowl and partridge, etc., etc., *ad infinitum*. Now he was retired and living in the district and would like to sample our local wildfowling. Could I? Would I? But of course — with pleasure; something really difficult? Well I did not know about that but I would do my best.

Late in the afternoon a day or two later, we waited in a creek on the curlews' flight line, the Sahib fortifying himself against the cold with occasional nips from a whisky flask. Being a teetotaller myself I wondered vaguely what effect this might have on his shooting, but my companion seemed to regard this as perfectly normal, so I was content to wait and see. In due course an orderly line of birds came winging down-river, the first of the curlew flight. As anticipated, they cut the corner of the merse *en route* for their roosting place on the sands and headed straight for us; the Sahib picked up his gun and prepared to do battle! Cautioning him to remain hidden until the last possible moment, I waited until the curlew were almost on top of us and called out ... "Now! "

The Sahib stood up and with nonchalant ease knocked down a right and left from the wildly finking curlew. It was a masterly performance, and I looked at my companion with renewed interest and respect. This had been a testing opening, as I could think of nothing more difficult to hit than curlew taking violent avoiding action. Could it have been something of a fluke, I wondered? The Sahib certainly didn't appear to think so, but he evidently did think it rated another little nip from the flask!

Stuck in the mud

Hardly had these birds been retrieved when another party of curlew appeared in the distance and again the Sahib prepared to receive the enemy. This lot came rather low, and somewhat to our right, and again, in spite of a wild swerve by the curlew, the Sahib had his two birds down. By now my admiration for him knew no bounds and I congratulated him most heartily. This he received without undue modesty, conceding that they were something difficult to shoot, particularly since his something feet were stuck in the something mud. Having commiserated with him about this and explained that in our brand of wildfowling one's feet were nearly always stuck in the mud, I stood back to watch the fun.

We had a splendid little flight and the Sahib was in great form, knocking them down right, left and centre. In order to give him full scope I did no shooting at all, but I have seldom enjoyed myself more. As dusk fell his shooting went off a little, but even so, when the flight ended, he had shot 16 curlew with just over 20 shots.

In the deepening dusk we moved out into the merse to try for duck. These proved to be few and far between, but I did manage to bag four wigeon from the two little companies that came my way. My companion had seen no duck, but just as we were packing up a pair of mallard appeared overhead and, although the Sahib missed with his first shot, he shot them both with his second, which rounded things off very nicely.

We decided to call it a day, and the flask having once again done its duty we set off for home. We had only a mile or so to go, but I will never forget that march across the merse as long as I live! The Sahib may well have been at home in the Indian jungle or even in the foothills, but a dark Scottish merse almost had him beaten! I did my best to light his way with the feeble beam from a little pocket flash-light, but despite this he found the going difficult, to say the least. Slipping and stumbling, splashing through deep, water-filled " puddles," the Sahib made his laborious way across the merse, stopping every now and then to roundly curse both it and myself for having brought him there. By the time we staggered over the cattle-bridge and across the fields to the car, the poor old Sahib was about all in, and a final pull at the flask was necessary to restore morale.

Nonetheless, about half-an-hour later he was assuring me that it had been one of the most enjoyable flights in which he had ever taken part and that "we must do this again sometime!" I think he really meant it at the time, but somehow I never did succeed in getting him out there again. Perhaps if we could have borrowed an elephant somewhere . . .?

RED LETTER DAY

AS the long grey punt slid down the mooring creek in the first light of dawn, we both experienced a wonderful sense of anticipation, almost of elation. Everything seemed set for a day of days. This was no ordinary outing, but had been planned and looked forward to for a long time. My friend and companion Pat, had recently acquired the punt and this, as far as we were concerned, was its maiden voyage.

Pat, whose home was in the south, had arrived at his cottage at the weekend, accompanied by one or two friends, having sent on in advance his 1½in. bore screw-breech puntgun, a first-class weapon that looked the acme of safety and efficiency. This was my first acquaintance with this gun and I was keen to see how it performed against the duck. I did not expect to have to wait very long. Already we knew the Gut held a number of wigeon, the whistling of the cocks having advised us of this as we launched the punt and loaded the big gun. Nearing the end of the creek we lay down and prepared for action—Pat at the gun and I in the setting position.

As we crept out into the river and the punt's head swung round to meet the ebb tide, it was immediately apparent that provided all went well we were going to have an excellent chance. Several hundred wigeon were in the Gut and although some were rather scattered on the water, the nearest birds were clustered thickly along the channel's edge. After a short but energetic push against the tide we were up to them. " What a chance," I thought, as Pat took careful aim and pulled the lanyard. With bated breath I waited for the crash of the shot—a faint click was the only result. With a rueful grin Pat looked over his shoulder, "misfire" he hissed. A quick glance at the duck past the side of the gun showed that their heads were up, and the nearest birds were swimming outwards, but there was still a chance. "Never mind," I whispered, " recock and try again." Pat did so, but again we were rewarded by a miserable click. " It's no use," he whispered back, " must be a dud cap, if you can work the punt backwards far enough to be clear of the duck I'll try to change the cartridge." Aided by the ebb tide I was able to do this without too much difficulty, and having opened up a sufficient distance, Pat set to work.

Lying as he was, flat on his face, and having to do everything without making the least noise, the change over proved a very awkward business. Panting and puffing with his exertions, he finally announced that he was once again ready for action. Fortunately our first attempt had disturbed only the birds in the lower reaches of the Gut, and these having swum upstream for some distance had once again gone ashore accompanied now by a large additional number of birds offering an even better chance than before.

In a very short time we were once again in range, surely nothing could go wrong this time. Again I held my breath as Pat sighted along the gun-barrel, seized the lanyard and pulled! Click! The sound, faint though it was, had almost the effect of a physical shock—another misfire ! We could scarcely believe it. This time the wigeon, thoroughly alarmed, took off with a roar of wings and vanished up river, leaving behind only a small company further up the Gut. After a brief discussion we decided to remain in the prone position, and if we could discover and cure the trouble we would have a go at this little lot. It was now clear enough to see quite well and before unloading the gun Pat examined the cartridge he had removed after the misfire ; the cap was almost unmarked—obviously the trouble lay in the striker mechanism. Removing the stock and unscrewing the breech-block my friend quickly discovered that the firing pin was

36

almost completely jammed by grease which had become hardened by the frost. Having freed the firing pin and reloaded the gun we set off to try conclusions with the 30 or so remaining wigeon. We were both disappointed at having missed such a splendid chance, but the day was young and we were hopeful of redeeming the situation sooner or later. We had little difficulty in getting up to the wigeon which were now spread out rather thinly, offering only a poor chance. The gun of course went off like 1 o'clock, and when the smoke cleared nine wigeon lay dead along the tide's edge.

Following the pick-up, we cleaned and reloaded the big gun and had only just got everything ship-shape when a company of about 150 wigeon hove in sight heading down river towards us. Hastily we lay down hoping that the duck would pitch either in the Gut or the main river channel where we could get at them with the punt. Instead of doing this however, they flew up on to the merse and after circling around for a time pitched quite close to a large creek that entered the river almost opposite where we lay in the punt. Confident that the wigeon would soon return to the river, we waited in readiness for an immediate attack.

The duck must have been very hungry however, for although we saw them once or twice during the next hour or so, when they made short flights, they always returned to the same area and again pitched on the grass. Finally we decided that the only way to get at them was to take our 12-bores and stalk them along the creek. There was no great difficulty about this as we were completely hidden from the duck while they were on the ground, and the creek itself was deep enough to enable us to walk almost upright for at least part of the way. Rowing across the river we anchored the punt at the creek mouth, loaded our guns and commenced the stalk. We had only gone a very short distance when to our intense disgust a low flying aircraft came roaring up the bay, and not surprisingly the wigeon took off. Flying off across the merse, the duck milled around for a time and finally having got over their fright headed straight back towards us. This time they pitched less than 150 yards from where we crouched, and after exchanging a few whispered words we carried on cautiously up the creek, I in the lead and Pat ploughing along through the soft mud in the rear.

When we thought we were directly opposite the wigeon we halted, and after taking a short breather scrambled on to a grassy ledge. Kneeling on this we slowly straightened up ; we had come a little too far but the wigeon were within easy range, feeding in a dense mass about 3o yards to our left. As the ducks' heads came up, our gun barrels simultaneously swung to the left—an instant later the birds jumped! Our volley caught them at the top of their jump and for a moment or two it literally rained duck as an astonishing number fell back on to the grass. Standing upright we watched the survivors of the company as they flew off down the merse edge. One after the other we saw two birds fall apparently dead and a third bank suddenly and go zooming down into the river.

Leaving Pat to deal with the runners at the scene of the fray, I hurried off after the droppers. The first two were, as we had thought, stone dead, and were picked up without any trouble, but the third was sitting out on the water looking very lively indeed. It was, I judged, just within range, so reloading the gun I aimed at its head and fired. The shot splashed all round the duck without having any apparent effect. Again I fired, but still the wigeon bobbed in the water untouched. Puzzled and none too pleased with my performance I was in the act of reloading when Pat arrived panting on the scene. " Can't you reach it ? " he asked, with a grin. " No, " I replied, " my shot doesn't seem to be having any effect." " Well these will," remarked Pat, slipping a couple of three inch cartridges into the chambers of his magnum. Again the shot splashed exactly on the mark and again the duck sat apparently untouched. " Well I'm blowed ! " exclaimed Pat in astonishment, and was about to shoot again when I noticed that the duck was slowly but surely drifting closer to us. " Don't shoot," I cried, " I believe that duck is dead, and what's more I think it has been dead all along."

This proved to be the case and soon afterwards the onshore wind drifted the bird to the water's edge. It was still sitting in the exact position of a swimming duck when we picked it up, and we both agreed that so far as we knew, this was the only instance of either of us shooting at a bird already dead in the belief that it was a live cripple. As we made our way back to the scene of the stalk I asked Pat how many wigeon we had shot, " I didn't count them," he replied, " but I reckon there's not far short of 20 back there, it was absolutely fantastic the way they rained down ! " The duck were lying in a heap where Pat had left them. We counted them—there were 24 duck in that pile ! These, with the three droppers made a total of 27 wigeon for our four barrel volley—we were flabbergasted!

Grinning at each other across the heap, we discussed the effect the news of this coup would have on the others when we forgathered in Pat's cottage later that day. " I foresee one difficulty about this," he remarked, " the others will never believe we shot this lot with one volley from the 12-bores, particularly since we set out on a punting expedition, they'll think we're shooting a line." I agreed wholeheartedly, but hoped we might be able to convince them. Little did either of us guess that an event taking place only a few miles away was going to make our story sound even less credible than we thought.

For us the rest of the morning was fairly quiet although we did manage to bag one more duck, a mallard. When we arrived home at Pat's cottage in the late afternoon, we found the others there before us. Although bursting to tell of our famous stalk, Pat, as became a good host, asked the others how they had fared. " Well, " replied Julian, " you're going to find this rather hard to believe, but old Bob and I stalked a party of wigeon this morning and shot fourteen with a four barrel volley!"

Ferryman recalls a rather close shave

QUICKSAND ! The very word is sufficient to send a shiver of horror through most people, and indeed it is difficult to imagine a more frightful end than to be slowly engulfed in semi-liquid sand or mud, or held prisoner in its remorseless grip until the incoming tide puts an end to the victim's misery and despair.

Fortunately, in this country fatal accidents of this nature involving human beings appear to be few and far between, but narrow escapes from just such a fearful death are by no means rare. Several have occurred in our own estuary, and an account of one such incident appears in Peter Scott's book " Morning Flight." I have good reason to sympathise with the person involved in this terrifying experience as I, myself, got into difficulties close to the scene of this event. There was, however, an important difference. Whereas Scott's friend was alone and could look to no one for help in his dreadful predicament, I was never in any comparable danger, furthermore, I was used to traversing soft sand and mud, and it is quite probable that I might have been able to extricate myself even if no help had been at hand. Nonetheless, I look back on that particular adventure with no pleasure at all !

It all began when my friend Angus and I planned a shoot at the " Big Puddles," a series of long, shallow water-holes situated close to the river's edge on a narrow strip of merseland. A reconnaissance in the morning had revealed that the area was liberally strewn with droppings, indicating that " The Puddles " were being used by wigeon, and since there was every prospect of someone else discovering this we decided to take advantage of our knowledge that very night. As dusk fell we took up our positions, each in a separate creek a couple of hundred yards apart. To my left front lay one of the water-holes, while on my right the mud sloped down to the river-bed, levelling off for about 60 yards before reaching the water. Almost at once small parties of curlew began flighting, and Angus, who was right on this line, had several shots, two of which were successful.

My first chance was at a single teal which pitched momentarily in one of the pools. As it took off again and came past me on my right it showed clearly against the sunset glow in the western sky, and fell to my shot, landing about half-way out on the mud flat of the river-bed. Since it was obviously dead I left it for the time being. Shortly afterwards three wigeon appeared as if by magic and were sweeping towards the pool when the shot from my single 12-bore caught the middle bird, which fell with a splash into the shallow water. Being uncertain whether or not this bird was dead, I hastily reloaded and climbed out of the creek to retrieve it. As I did so Angus's gun went off twice. Kneeling on one knee I gazed eagerly into the pink-flushed sky and a moment later a little party of wigeon flashed across my front, heading out towards the river. A quick snap shot into the " brown " and I saw one bird drop out of the company and heard a thud as it hit the mud of the sloping bank. After retrieving the wigeon which had dropped in the water-hole I hurried down the sloping mud and, after a brief search, found the second wigeon lying stone-dead at the bottom.

The teal I had shot earlier lay only a short distance away and was faintly visible as a dark blob on the smooth mud-flat, so leaving the two wigeon lying on the firm mud at the bottom of the slope, I set out to retrieve it. The sand-cum-mud flats in this part of the river have always to be treated with respect. I knew the mud would be soft, but by using the local method of moving quickly and without pause I expected to be able to pick up the duck without much trouble. It was something of a shock therefore to find by the time I had covered a little over half the distance, that I was plunging in so deeply I could scarcely lift my feet high enough to take another step. Although not unduly alarmed, I decided it was too dangerous to continue and at once commenced making a " U " turn in order to regain the firm mud again as quickly as possible. I would probably have succeeded in this but at that point my right foot pulled up into the leg of my sea-boot; this stopped me in my tracks. Within seconds I was almost hip-deep in the mud, so without hesitation I fell forward until I was lying face downward, my gun under me to give me some slight support. By dint of vigorous wriggling I succeeded in getting my foot back into its proper place in the boot, and paused to consider my next move.

One thing was certain, I was not going to *walk* out of this lot. The alternatives were to crawl or roll out, but before attempting either, it was essential to get my legs clear and my body as nearly as possible on a horizontal plane. This was easier said than done and my attempts to extricate my legs quickly convinced me that if I were to succeed unaided it would almost certainly have to be at the expense of my sea-boots, and perhaps my gun as well. I decided to call for help. "Angus " I shouted, " Angus ahoy ! I'm stuck ! " Holding my breath I listened carefully and somewhat anxiously for a reply, —nothing, —only the sigh of the cold east wind. Again and again I shouted at the top of my voice, a slow and unreasoning anger building up in me. "Where the devil was the fellow ?" " Why didn't he come, or at least answer me ?" " Surely he must realise I wouldn't be bellowing like this for nothing !" I felt resentment and a ridiculous feeling of self-pity rising in me, and then suddenly there he was, walking quickly down the sloping mud-bank. A wave of intense relief swept over me and immediately everything was back to normal.

" Angus I'm stuck," I called, " don't come beyond the bottom of the slope, it's much too soft."

" Are you all right ?" he asked anxiously. " What do you want me to do—do you want me to go along to the farm for a rope ?"

" No, no," I replied, " things aren't as bad as all that, in any case it would take too long, and the tide's due almost any time now. There's an old broken-down fence only a short distance up the merse from here ; you should be able to break off a length of fencing wire, and that will serve just as well."

" Right-o," replied my friend, " I know where it is, now don't worry, I'll be back as soon as I can." He hurried back up the slope, and disappeared over the top, leaving me alone once more.

I took stock of the situation. My action in lying bent forward from the hips had been effective in preventing my legs sinking much deeper, but they were as firmly trapped as ever. A tentative attempt at wriggling forward only resulted in the mud becoming churned up and the gun on which I was leaning being pushed deeper into the glutinous stuff. Until I had something to pull on it was obviously going to be impossible to get my legs free without pulling them out of my sea-boots. Having done this, I felt sure I could then manage to crawl or roll out, but I was reluctant to do so unless it became absolutely necessary, and since there was still no sign of the tide, I decided to wait with whatever patience I could muster, for Angus's return.

The wait seemed longer than I had hoped for, but eventually he came loping over the edge of the bank carrying a fence post, and trailing behind him a long length of wire which was attached to it. Making a loop in the end of the wire, Angus, after several unsuccessful attempts, finally succeeded in pushing it within my reach. He then wriggled the post about half its length into the clay, pulled in the slack of the wire, and announced that he was ready. Pulling with all my strength on the wire loop I gradually worked my legs free, and then, rolling over on my side managed, with some difficulty, to extricate the gun from the mud. Turning again on my face, I pulled myself along the wire until I was able to stand up on reasonably firm mud.

" I was out ! "

Plastered with mud from head to foot but safe, sound, and very thankful ! After washing off the worst of the mud in a nearby pool, we decided to call it a day, and headed for home. The little teal lay where it had fallen!

THE MORNING OF THE GOLDENEYE

A very good one, recalls Ferryman

THE car bumped to a halt at the end of the rough sandy track, and as I climbed out the first faint finger of dawn streaked the sky to eastward. Almost at once I heard mallard quacking in the little river close by, and made haste to get into my fowling rig. A few minutes later, loaded like a camel with gear which included rubber decoys, a plastic bucket, a garden spade and a sack of seaweed (previously gathered along the tidemark) I crunched down the beach and set out across the sand and shingle flats towards the bend in the river where I intended to make my hide.

This little estuary, although sometimes favoured by a considerable number of duck, was extremely difficult to shoot since there was virtually no natural cover of any sort. On our one previous visit my son and I had attempted to get over this difficulty by scraping shallow holes in the shingle banks, and crouching in these, had contrived to knock down a few duck. The holes had to be shallow as deep ones immediately filled with water and even shallow trenches had to be baled out at intervals. Nevertheless, it was obvious to us that the place had possibilities, and although my son could not accompany me on this occasion, I determined to try once again. On arrival at the selected spot, a bank of rough shingle at a slight bend in the river, I dumped my load and set to work with the spade. Soon I had scooped out a roughly circular hole about a couple of feet deep, banking the excavated shingle round the perimeter, and augmenting this with more shingle shovelled from outside the hole. Even this shallow pit began to collect water, but I felt that with the aid of my bucket I could easily keep it in check. Finally I added the seaweed to the top of this bank and found that by kneeling in the hole and crouching like a hare, I could just keep my head below the level of the " parapet." Next, although it was still much too dark for them to be seen, I floated my decoys in a little fleet about 30 yards upstream, loaded the magnum and settled down to wait.

By now the lowering sky had taken on a greyish tingle and a strong and " Snell " wind blew in from the sea. Suddenly a single duck appeared out of the murk, flying low above the river, and vanished seaward before I could get the gun to my shoulder. Seconds later four more duck appeared at almost the same height, and the one quick shot I managed as they disappeared into the gloom was followed by a splash. This proved to be a duck mallard.

During the next ten minutes or so several small parties of mallard flew past, but the duck were so low and the light so bad that I simply couldn't hit them. I must have fired six or eight ineffective shots before I again connected. This time it was a pair of wigeon, straight overhead and much easier to see ; my right and left was on the mark and as the shots struck home the duck appeared to remain stationary for a brief moment and then grow larger and larger as they plummeted down almost on top of me. This success restored my confidence somewhat and shortly afterwards, when a single duck which I took to be a wigeon, appeared out of the gloom, I brought it down with a splash right in the middle of the river. Wading out through the shallow water I retrieved the duck, and on returning to my hide was surprised and annoyed to find I had shot a goldeneye, a species I would not normally have attempted to shoot.

Shortly after this event the light improved to such an extent that my decoys had obviously become visible, and a little party of five wigeon would have pitched in the river if I had let them. My first shot missed but my second brought a cock splashing down among the decoys. I was just about to retrieve this bird when two more wigeon appeared, and crouching down in the hide I let them come right up. When I rose to take the shot the wigeon flared and blew to leeward at a terrific pace. Again I missed with my first shot and again my second brought a bird down, this time well out on the shingle on the far side of the river. Since I was uncertain whether or not this bird was dead, I waded across after it, picking up *en route* the wigeon that had fallen among the decoys. On reaching the far side I discovered that the remaining duck was only winged, but after a short chase I secured it and was just about to recross the river when I spotted two more wigeon approaching. Sitting down on the shingle and making myself as inconspicuous as possible I watched the duck out of the corner of my eye. To my surprise they took no notice of me, their attention being centred on the decoys.

Still as a mouse I waited until they were as close as they were ever likely to be and then, still seated, I uncoiled and swung on them. They dropped one after the other into the river, a right and left to be remembered for a long time.

Returning to the hide I was just in time to spot a single mallard drake heading down-river towards me. This bird took no apparent notice of the decoys, and as he passed at point-blank range, I missed him handsomely with both barrels! Cursing under my breath, I was in the act of reloading when three more mallard, two drakes and a duck, appeared on the same track. Well, thank goodness, I thought, here was a chance to redeem myself. I would shoot the two drakes and spare the duck. Alas and alack! Again I clean missed the bird I aimed at, probably because I fired while still crouched on both knees, a position not conducive to good shooting.

Disgusted with myself for having muffed two easy chances, I determined that if anything else came I would stand up to shoot. However, fate in the first instance decreed otherwise. While watching some distant birds that I thought might be duck, I was "snuck up on " by three teal which were almost on top of me before I saw them. These duck were coming down-wind and were travelling at a tremendous pace. Without changing my position I swung ahead of the leading bird—a mighty swing—and he was dead in the air. So also was the last bird to my second shot, and they hit the shingle side by side, a long way from the hide. Delighted with my change of fortune I renewed my watch. It was now almost broad daylight and I began to fear that sport might be over for the day, but just as hope faded, eight duck in a tight little pack appeared from seaward. At first I thought they were wigeon but soon the white cheek patches and wing bars proclaimed them to be goldeneye. Flashing past on whistling wings, they turned into the wind and in a twinkling splashed down into the river close beside the decoys.

After sitting on the water for a few moments they rose and flew past within a few yards of the hide. During the next half hour or so these birds, or others of their kind, passed up-or down-river several times, twice more pitching briefly beside the decoys and giving me a splendid opportunity to observe them. During this period I added five more duck to the bag, two mallard and three wigeon, two of the latter being another right and left at a pair. Despite some very bad shooting I ended this most interesting and enjoyable morning with 11 wigeon, three mallard, two teal and the unfortunate goldeneye. By my standards, a very good morning indeed.

THE entry in my game book reads, " Place—B . . . Island, guns 1 (self), mallard 3, teal 4, Various One 20 lb. plus Cod !" Mind you, I admit I cheated a little over this entry, as I did not actually *shoot* the cod—and thereby, of course, hangs a tale!

B . . . Island is, at first sight, a most unlikely looking place for duck. Quite small and completely rock girt, its foreshores consist of formidable reefs, most of them covered with masses of bladder-wrack. On the leeward side the shore shelves off less steeply, forming a sort of rocky tongue, with little bays at either end. As the

MIXED BAG

An odd morning's sport described by Ferryman

A team of four mallard passed close inshore of me.   Pamela Harrison

tide ebbs, shallow water-holes are left behind the reefs on this tongue, and these are surprisingly attractive to duck. On occasion a fair number of mallard, teal and sometimes wigeon visit the island, and I have even shot geese here once or twice. The island is seldom without interest, great rafts of scoter frequent the vicinity, and the distant sound of their voices, peculiarly unducklike, is characteristic of the place. These duck remain out at sea, however, rarely venturing close inshore. Occasionally a common seal will pop its head out of the sea within a few yards of one, and after a brief scrutiny sink back into the tangle-grown depth.

On the morning in question I arrived opposite the island in the drizzly darkness of pre-dawn, picked my way carefully across the rocky neck connecting the island to the mainland, and then round the shoulder of the island to the little rock bay where I intended awaiting the hoped-for flight. The latter part of the journey is difficult in the extreme, the going being very rough and slippery, and great care is necessary to avoid injury to oneself or damage to one's gun. Having arrived safely, I put out a couple of rubber mallard decoys, floating them as far out as I could wade, which wasn't very far, as the shore at this point shelves steeply, and at low tide it is impossible to take more than a step or two seaward. This is a serious drawback, and unless one has a dog, which at present I have not, one can only shoot at birds either over, or very close to the shore, or run the risk of losing them in the sea.

The first arrivals were four mallard which pitched on the water directly in front of me, but although they were within range, it was still too dark to see them without the aid of the binoculars. Indeed, I had been quite unaware of their arrival until a movement I made caused the rubber duck call, which was hanging round my neck, to " quack." This was immediately echoed by a mallard duck which set up a vigorous quacking. I decided to do nothing about them until the light improved, but, unfortunately, this was one of those mornings with a dense overcast, when night yields to day slowly and reluctantly. Shortly after this the duck began to flight in earnest and if the light had been better I would have had many chances. As it was, I caught only an occasional fleeting glimpse of the flighting duck and it wasn't until a party of about a dozen teal swept in from seaward that I got my first shot. As the duck flashed past on my right I got off one shot just before they vanished against the black loom of the island, and saw the bird slant down towards one of the water holes. Hastily reloading, I looked around for any of the early arrivals my shot might have put up. Sure enough, in the next minute or two, several parties of mallard and teal flew past, almost all within range, but all out over the sea where I was unable, or at any rate reluctant, to shoot them.

Soon afterwards I heard a duck mallard quacking and spotted a pair heading inshore on my left—a shake of the duck call and they turned straight towards me. I let them go right past to where I could see them best against the lightening sky and then fired at the rearmost bird which splashed into the sea a few yards out. My second shot at the remaining bird apparently missed, so propping the gun against a rock, I scrambled down the water's edge to retrieve the fallen duck. This I succeeded in doing by the " string and stick " method, having as always the necessary items in my gamebag. These consist of a piece of buoyant wood at least 18 inches long, to each end of which is tied a piece of string, forming as it were, a bow with a very slack bow-string. The end of a long ball of string is then tied to the middle of the " bow-string," sufficient slack coiled in the left hand and the stick thrown over and beyond the floating bird. If the aim is good it is only necessary to pull gently on the string until the wood is in contact with the bird, which can then be pulled ashore. If the aim is not so good and the wood is beyond the bird but not in line with it, the desired result can often be achieved by moving along the shore in the appropriate direction until the string passes directly over the floating duck. If the string is then held as low as possible, the pressure will often be found sufficient to bring the bird ashore.

During the few minutes taken to retrieve the duck, at least two excellent chances went a-begging, one at a team of four mallard which passed close inshore of me, and another at a party of teal which whizzed right over my head. As so often happens on these occasions, when I was once again back in my stance and ready to receive all comers, the only duck I saw for a considerable time was a bunch of mallard which pitched on the sea behind some outlying rocks. Although I quacked at them with my call they took no notice, but my efforts were not in vain, for a pair of mallard, the duck quacking like mad, appeared from nowhere and as they crossed my front I killed them both with a right and left. Leaving them for the time being, I reloaded just in time to drop a single teal into the sea. This bird was rather a long way out, just a little too far to reach with the " stick," though I tried one or two throws. The wind, however, was now freshening and as it was blowing directly on to the mainland, I thought I would have a good chance of picking up the teal when it eventually drifted ashore.

Picking up the two dead mallard I returned to my stance and resumed my watch. Several other parties of duck, both mallard and teal, appeared shortly after this but all of them pitched well out to sea. It was now broad daylight and looked as though the flight was over for the day. The tide was rapidly covering the outlying rocks and in a little over half an hour or so the island would be cut off. It was time to go !

I was in the act of packing up when I spotted seven teal approaching. These duck were flying parallel to the island, about 25 yards out over the sea, too far to reach with the " stick." Well, I had one duck to search for on the mainland, why not another ? When they were directly opposite I fired, killing one with each barrel. Gathering up my gear I set out to look for the teal which had fallen in the water-hole earlier on. I was none too confident of finding this duck as I knew from experience that a bird, not carefully marked, was notoriously difficult to find amongst the seaweed-covered rocks, so on nearing the place where I thought it had come down I was relieved to see something moving in the shallow water behind a reef. " Ah ! the teal," I thought, " and still alive, too." Putting down my gamebag I approached warily, gun at the ready, in case it should jump me at the last moment. To my astonishment I discovered that the movement was caused by the tail of a huge fish that had evidently become trapped behind the reef as the tide dropped. The fish, a cod, was at its last gasp, being so large that it was only partially submerged, so grabbing it by the tail I hauled it out of the pool and hit it on the head with my " throwing stick." After gutting it and cutting off its huge head, I put the remainder in a polythene bag and continued my hunt for the teal.

After a careful search among the rocks I found it lying dead and already stiff—a beautiful little cock. A look through the binoculars now revealed that the three remaining teal had already drifted almost halfway to the mainland, so, anxious to be there before they reached the rocks, I set off as fast as I could safely go. It was touch and go, but I made it just in time to spot each of them as they washed ashore at surprisingly wide intervals, and also to drive off, with an out-of-range shot, a greater black-backed gull that had discovered one of the teal and was about to make a meal of it.

On arriving home, the fish, minus the head, etc., was found to weigh almost 15 lb. so originally it must have weighed well over 20 lb. An unexpected but eery acceptable bonus.

Fowlers Progress

Ferryman harks back to Shank's, James and Nippy

I was ruminating on the subject of coastal journeys one morning last season as we sped in the early hours in the warm comfort of a modern car, towards one of our more distant fowling grounds. As the rain lashed down with such force that the screen wipers could barely cope with it, I conjured up a vision of my friend Bob and I on just such a morning many years ago, slowly forging ahead on a couple of pedal bikes, our guns and bags slung across our backs, bound for a goose flight 13 miles away.

At times we were blown almost to a standstill, and so hard was the going that by the time we reached the farm where the bikes were abandoned and shank's mare resorted to, dawn had already broken. As we splashed and slithered our way at our best speed across the muddy field that lay between the farm and the merse edge, we heard the distant voices of geese as they lifted off the high sands and headed inshore. Judging by the sound they appeared to be crossing the merse on almost exactly the line we had hoped they would use, and where we had intended to lie in wait for them. We were bitterly disappointed at arriving too late, but pressed on regardless, and soon were scrambling over the stile onto the merse, pausing only long enough to push a couple of BBs into the chambers of our guns.

A short distance ahead lay the cattle bridge that spanned the "Judge's Burn". We headed for the bridge and had covered about half the distance when we heard the clamour of approaching geese. Breaking into a run we made for the bridge at top speed and arrived panting and breathless just as a wavering line of greylags appeared out of the murk heading straight for us. We crouched in the shelter of the bridge railings, one at each side, our hearts beating like sledge-hammers, and I heard two clicks as Bob thumbed back the hammers of his gun. I cocked my own and changed my position slightly as the geese appeared to be veering somewhat to our right. As I moved, water from my sou-wester cascaded into my eyes and I was momentarily blinded. A moment later the geese were on us and Bob, who was always "faster", had both barrels off before I fired my first shot. As I aimed very deliberately at the goose I had chosen, I saw one bird fall from the skein. At my shot my goose crumpled up and plummeted to the ground. I swung onto the next bird and fired instantly; this bird followed the first one down. Bob's yell of triumph was echoed by my own

When the road is covered with ice or rutted frozen snow I am often reminded of some of our escapades on the old motor bike that Bob eventually acquired. This infamous machine, which gloried in the name of " James ", had to be petted, cossetted and often pushed before it would deign to start, and even then there was always a grave doubt about this happening. Nevertheless its advent opened up vistas previously undreamed of, and we thought nothing of setting out on long journeys over roads often ice or snow-bound, to some out of the way fowling spot. That we would come to grief sooner or later was a matter of certainty, and since I, being the pillion rider, was obliged to carry both guns slung over my shoulders, I had to develop a technique of falling off without damaging the guns. Astonishing to relate, despite many spills and not a few bruises, no damage was ever done to the guns on these occasions.

Some time later came the era of "Nippy"! Nippy was a tiny two-seater sports car, and was long past its best when it came within our ken. It was the pride and joy of our friend H. of whom I have written previously, and I well remember how impressed we were when he arrived home with this wonderful vehicle. My brother Jack and I, having no free time until the following Saturday afternoon, it was arranged that all three of us would then travel in Nippy to a merse on the opposite side of our estuary for evening flight. This was doing things in style and we were immensely proud and happy to be travelling in such a fine car. Saturday could not come soon enough!

In due course H. in full fowling rig, drove round to the house, remarking as we loaded the guns and other gear into the tiny space behind the seats that " she wasn't going too well ". Having had no experience of cars, neither my brother or myself paid a great deal of attention to this remark, being far too much in love with Nippy. Soon we were on the road and heading, if somewhat slowly, towards the market town through which we had to pass *en route* to our fowling grounds. Our arrival in the town caused something of a stir, which was hardly surprising. The tiny car was literally crammed with three oddly dressed young men, one of whom was perched high on top of the folded down hood, there being nowhere else to sit. Sticking upwards from the back were the barrels of four guns, including a single 8-bore we had brought along in case we encountered any geese. We were definitely something out of the ordinary!

Amidst many smiles and much head turning, we drove slowly through the busy streets; all went well until we came to a steep hill right in the middle of the town. Before we were half-way up, Nippy's speed had dropped alarmingly, and soon she ground to a halt—something to do with the clutch we were informed. Nothing else for it but to climb overboard and push, while H. coaxed whatever he could get out of the "works". This was embarrassing to say the least, and as we panted slowly uphill amidst the smiles and ribald remarks of passers-by, we were horribly conscious of the name Nippy painted in large letters along each side of the car! She had let us down badly !

Even though we eventually reached our destination safely and had a most enjoyable flight, Nippy had another shock in store for us when we set out on the return journey. After travelling only a few miles her lights grew dimmer and dimmer, and we finished the journey with myself sitting on a mudguard, shining an electric torch on the road verge to enable H. to steer. It is probably unnecessary to add that the era of Nippy, though eventful, was quite brief.

. . . the geese were on us . . .

Pamela Harriswon

THE WAYS OF
A PEREGRINE

FOR a number of years, in common with many other parts of Britain, the peregrine population of this district of Scotland has shown a serious, almost catastrophic decline, and breeding success has been very low indeed. The possible causes of this state of affairs have been thoroughly ventilated, and perhaps it will suffice to say that there now appears little doubt that the ingestion of certain agricultural pesticides, which have accumulated in the bodies of their prey, is the prime factor.

Having always been thrilled and fascinated by these magnificent and aristocratic birds, the sight of so many deserted eyries

. . . magnificent and aristocratic birds   *Eric Hoshing*

has been for me a very saddening one. It has therefore been with great pleasure that I have recently noted peregrines in the vicinity of several traditional nesting sites and have high hopes of the beginning of a cycle of recovery. Not far from my home a couple of peregrines used to breed regularly on a sea-cliff, the eyrie usually being situated on a ledge close to the entrance to a large " pigeon cave," yet despite the close proximity of their terrible enemy, there was a constant stream of rock doves in or out of this and other nearby caves and crevices. Oddly enough, I never once saw the peregrines kill one of these doves, and only rarely found remains at the " plucking place," but on one occasion I saw the female of this couple shoot out from the ledge where she had been incubating four eggs and strike and kill one of a flock of jackdaws which were doing aerial " squad drill " in front of the cliff. This unfortunate bird fell about 100 feet into the sea, the falcon making no attempt to catch or retrieve it, having apparently attacked in order to drive the jackdaws away. In this she was only temporarily successful as the jackdaws were quickly back on the scene. This behaviour was, of course, typical of jackdaws, as nothing except death will shift these birds from a cliff once they have colonised it.

Of all British raptors, peregrines probably show the greatest variation in size and colour. Some of the large, lighter coloured falcons are in sharp contrast to their smaller and often much darker kin. Likewise they vary greatly in temperament and, apparently, in courage. Sometimes a falcon will slip quietly off the nest, and even if it contains young, will start calling only from a considerable distance, while another, and perhaps her mate as well, will remain close to the eyrie screaming with rage and " dive-bombing " like mad. At one such eyrie where we did some filming, the falcon constantly attacked, shooting down the cliff face in a series of screaming dives, sometimes passing so close to our heads that each time we involuntarily ducked as her screams sounded almost in our ears. Fortunately for us she never drove home any of these attacks which were designed to scare us off, and very nearly did! Her mate, too, was a very aggressive bird, and in the vicinity of this eyrie there was seldom a dull moment.

The eyrie was situated at no great distance from a large farm, the owner and his workers being well aware of its existence. The farm foreman told us that the falcons had taken almost all his tame pigeons, sometimes close to the farm buildings. The pigeons used to perch on the roof of his cottage and the peregrines were seen on several occasions to put the pigeons on the wing by making a dummy attack and then strike and kill one in mid-air. It says a lot for human forebearance that this chap accepted this as natural and inevitable and neither he nor anybody else in the district took any aggressive action against these birds which nested successfully in the same site for many years.

An eyass (young falcon), reared by this couple, taught me something of the steely strength of a peregrine's talons. I was present when the youngster attempted its first flight from the ledge upon which it had been reared. Taking wing, the eyass flew out over the sea losing height steadily, until apparently aware of its danger, it turned back towards the cliffs. The distance, however, was too great and to my distress the bird crashed into the sea about 60 yards short of the cliffs. I watched anxiously, fearful that it would drown, when to my delight it proceeded to swim ashore using its wings as paddles. Having lost sight of the eyass just before it reached the cliff bottom, I was still anxious about its safety and decided to descend the cliff and, if possible, capture it and return it to the nesting ledge. With the aid of a rope I descended the near vertical cliff and eventually spotted the youngster, wet and bedraggled, sitting on a narrow ledge just out of reach of the sea. Working my way slowly and carefully along the cliff foot I approached the bird, which made no attempt to escape, apparently having had its fill of flying for the time being. Holding the rope with one hand, I reached out with the other towards the eyass which sat regarding me with its huge and already fierce eyes. My intention was to grab it and tuck it somehow inside my jersey for the return trip up the cliff. My hand had almost closed on the youngster when it suddenly flipped over onto its back and struck like lightning with its talons. A sharp pain shot through my hand and an attempt to snatch it away brought the bird with it, one of its talons being firmly embedded in my thumb! This was not what I had planned but at any rate it solved the problem of transport as the eyass was now firmly anchored, and I climbed back up the cliff with it clinging to my hand and blood dripping all over the place.

On arrival at the top I disengaged the talon from my thumb, shot a few feet of film and returned the youngster to the eyrie. All this time I had been under almost constant attack by the parent falcon, which kept stooping at my head in a most alarming fashion. This particular female was by far the boldest and fiercest peregrine I ever encountered, and was the only bird of her kind to cause uneasiness by the closeness of her attacks. Sad to say, she is no longer with us, but we look forward to the day when her place will be taken by another of her kind.

STORM FLIGHT

A morning of excitement, interest and first-class shooting described by Ferryman

WHEN the alarm went off at 4 a.m. that morning, the sound of the wind and rain was audible, even above its strident clamour. Not that the other interested member of the family heard anything of this until callously nudged awake, which was hardly surprising, since he, our son and heir, had driven over 200 miles the previous day to join his friend Hugh and I at morning flight.

Now wind is a thing we like and, indeed, to ensure success it is a thing we need, and when someone has travelled 200 miles for just one flight it is something to be hoped, whistled and prayed for. When we had turned in five hours previously, the night, although cloudy had been calm and peaceful, So we had hoped and whistled and prayed. But wind *and* rain, ah! Here was a different kettle of fish. A quick peep past the curtains revealed a lashing storm-driven downpour, and we felt vaguely let down, somebody, somewhere had overdone it!

Less than an hour later we were well on our way to the chosen spot, having picked up Howard's friend Hugh in a neighbouring town *en route*. Making good time over the rain-swept roads, we arrived near the scene of action with some time to spare and, reluctant to leave the warm, dry comfort of the car for the stormy darkness, we decided to wait as long as possible before venturing forth. The car, broadside on to the wind, rocked and swayed as we peered out, watching the sullen sky for the first sign of dawn. Suddenly the heavens opened and the rain, heavy enough before in all conscience, fell on the car roof in a roaring deluge. "Well" remarked Hugh, in an attempt at levity, "that's the 'uplifting shower'—it'll be dry in about 10 minutes!" There's many a true word spoken in jest—in about the time predicted, the wind, although still blowing as hard as ever, had shifted a couple of points, and the rain, now considerably abated, showed obvious signs of drying up. Scrambling out of the car in high spirits, we donned our fowling gear and set out in the teeth of the gale across the sand and shingle flats to the riverside flight-line.

On arrival at our destination we found the tide much higher than we had expected, the wind straight off the sea having pushed the water up the estuary to such an extent, that with the better part of an hour still to go, the tide was already past the normal neap tide high water mark. This, combined with the rain-swollen flood pouring down the river, made it impossible for us to use the riverside shingle bank upon which we had planned to construct our hides. We decided, therefore, to construct them on a shingle bank some way back from the river, using as building material some of the masses of seaweed lying around. The one snag was that the only area now available to us was a fairly narrow one, so to avoid danger, it was arranged that the boys should share a single hide, while I would occupy a second one a safe distance away.

Passed on either side

The construction of the hides kept us busy for quite a while and by the time we were ready for action the grey light of dawn had begun to penetrate the heavy storm clouds overhead. Almost at once my son Howard had a snap-shot at a single duck, momentarily glimpsed against the sky, but apparently missed. Shortly afterwards, as the light improved, small parties of duck were seen battling against the wind as they headed seaward. Time and again, they appeared to be making straight for one or other of the hides and just as often, buffetted by the wind, they veered to the right or left, passing just out of range. By the time it was light enough to see clearly, scores of duck, mainly mallard, had passed us. All of these had been low enough to shoot, indeed most had been only a few yards high, yet by the time the flight finally ended, not another duck had come within fair range !

Daylight now revealed a sea churned into a foaming mass of breakers, white in the offing and yeasty brown in our immediate vicinity where the flood water of the river forced its way out through the surf. Great sheets of spindrift, torn from the wave tops, raced across the surface and a continuous, stupendous roar dominated everything. One thing was obvious, no duck was going to sit out there very long and a return flight was an absolute certainty. I decided to hold a council of war with the boys.

As I made my way across to their hide, now only a few yards from the water's edge, they stood up, glad of the chance to straighten their legs. I had only just reached the hide, a piled-up ring of seaweed in which it was necessary to crouch like a hare in order to remain unseen, when Hugh spotted a pair of mallard heading in from the sea and coming straight at us. Down we got—I, being outside the hide, flattening myself against the outer wall. "Take them well in front," I called, " they're going at a tremendous rate." Seconds later two shots rang out almost simultaneously, and when I rolled over on to my back and looked up, both mallard were plummetting to earth. This was great stuff, and I was delighted at the boys' success, for these duck had been travelling just about as fast as they ever do, and anybody who has shot duck flying with the wind in their tails knows just how fast that is ! One of the boys retrieved the duck and I was just about to return to my own hide when three more mallard were spotted over the sea, heading our way.

" A cracking shot "

On they came, high and fast, and as they passed over, each of the boys got off one shot, and another mallard came crashing down, hitting the sand a very long way behind us. The boys laughed in high glee, each of them declaring he had fired at the same bird, which I have no doubt they did, as in any small party of duck there is usually one which looks more shootable than the others.

At that moment another mallard—a drake—headed our way, going like the others at a rate of knots but somewhat lower. At first it appeared likely to pass on the left of the hide, and the boys positioned themselves with this in view, but at the last moment it changed course and put them at a disadvantage. " Can you take him, dad ? " Howard called, "Hugh and I can't get round." Rising to my knees I looked up just as the drake came within range. I was facing in exactly the right direction, so without getting off my knees I took a mighty swing and he was " dead in the air." " A cracking shot dad," yelled Howard, above the roar of the surf, and the " old man " was secretly very pleased at not having let the side down. Picking up the mallard I hurried across to my own hide ; a considerable number of duck were now appearing from seaward, but, unfortunately, many of them were flying up the line of the river and disappearing inland, while others were flying along the tide edge to the other side of the estuary. Nevertheless there was constant interest, as duck were visible, somewhere or other, almost all the time, and storm-tossed parties of waders streamed past our hides, sometimes literally within a few feet of our heads. Among these were large flocks of knot and dunlin and smaller parties of turnstones, ringed-plovers and other waders. Parties of godwit were constantly on the move as were many redshank and curlew. We never shoot waders (except golden plovers) and were content to take this wonderful opportunity of watching these birds at close range.

High and fast

Twice a hunting peregrine flew past within gunshot, and several times we saw it attack parties of duck without any apparent success. Finally it stooped at and killed a pigeon after two unsuccessful attempts. The distance was too great to be quite sure, but we were reasonably certain that someone's pigeon loft would be a bird short as a result!

Eventually, a team of mallard headed our way, gradually gaining height as they neared the shore. So high and fast were they that as they passed over the boys' hide I was somewhat taken aback when four shots rang out, and incredibly there were three dead mallard blowing away to leeward like leaves in the gale. They struck the sand a long, long way behind us, and were among the highest and fastest flying duck I ever saw shot. Later, when we examined them, we found all three more or less damaged, two of them, both fine drakes, being split open along the breast-bone. After this only two more duck, a pair of wigeon, came within range, again over the boys' hide. In view of what had gone before, I wasn't in the least surprised to see both of them drop to the boys' shots, to complete a modest bag and round off a morning of great interest and excitement, and of first-class shooting by these young sportsmen. As we headed for the car, the wind on our backs pushing us along in good style, the salt on our lips tasted very sweet.

The Luck of the Game

Everything depended on the frost holding— or so Ferryman thought

I lost a first-class chance at five mallard.   Pamela Harrison

ON the east side of our estuary, a few miles from my home, lies a long, flat, stony stretch of shore locally known as the "Scaur." It is the haunt of vast numbers of waders, and in my younger days I spent many exciting and happy hours there, flighting the curlew and golden plover that often came to feed among the seaweed-covered stones as the ebbing tide revealed them.

From time to time the Scaur is visited by fair numbers of mallard, and occasionally by pintail, but it is very difficult to get on terms with these duck. This is due to the size of the area and the fact that, more often than not, they pitch in the tidal channel and swim inshore when the tide covers the Scaur, remaining behind as the water ebbs off. As a result, relatively few are shot each season, and it is therefore a matter of great satisfaction when one is able to outwit some of these crafty duck and come off the Scaur with a reasonable bag. Under certain conditions of tide and weather this can sometimes be done, particularly when hard frost coincides with high tides. At one end of the Scaur, a small burn meanders among the stones and mudflats, and in time of frost this often proves attractive to duck, provided the tides are high enough to prevent it freezing over. On the other hand, with a combination of frost and neap tides, the place is almost deserted, except perhaps for a few dozen oyster-catchers and other small waders.

One morning last season, during a sharp frost, I spied the area bright and early, and there, to my great satisfaction, sat between 40 and 50 mallard, most of them in or near the burn and a good many within range of the little stone butt we had built and used many times previously. Having the following day off work, I decided on an early morning attack and hoped devoutly that the frost would last at least one more day. The next morning, to my intense disgust, I awoke to a howling sou'-westerly gale and driving rain, but with the memory of all those fat mallard to spur me on I decided to continue. My car being unavailable, I set out in the teeth of the gale on my daughter's bike, making, I am afraid, rather heavy weather of the journey! When I got to the scene of action it was still very dark, but with the aid of the bike lamp I built up the butt, draping it liberally with seaweed and keeping its height to the bare minimum necessary to conceal me in the kneeling position. We had found from experience that a butt of this kind worked perfectly when built among seaweed-covered stones or shingle so long as its silhouette was kept low enough.

Shortly after I had everything organised, it grew a little lighter, and the curlew began to flight. The vast majority were flying right into the teeth of the wind, and were so low that they were quite invisible until they were almost on top of me. Other birds came and went, flights of piping oyster-catchers and various gulls, while carrion crows ghosted past, occasionally uttering their harsh croak, for the Scaur is a great place for these sable pests ; but time went on, the light increased and there was still no sign or sound of a duck. I began to feel somewhat dispirited and a conviction grew, which I stubbornly resisted, that the change in the weather had affected their recent routine and that I would see few if any duck that morning, and then . . . coming straight at me out of the gloom were four mallard! Unfortunately they pitched too soon, just a little too far out for a shot, so I let them be, and shortly afterwards three more passed across my front at long range, heading for the sea. I tried a shot at one of these, but it went on apparently unscathed. A moment later a single drake shot over my head at a height of a few yards ; he had come right down out of the fields on my "blind" side and was gone before I even got the gun up !

I was sitting fuming about this when it occurred to me that unless I kept a better look-out in that direction this could happen again. I looked over my right shoulder as the thought struck me, and there was a scattered bunch of about 16 to 20 mallard, coming across my front from right to left at about 40 yards ! I fired when they were straight in front of me, dropping two, a duck and a drake, with my first shot, and a duck with my second. Some time later three more came over, passing right overhead, rather high up and going like mad. I fired at the second bird—a drake—and hit him with both barrels, but he carried on for about 150 yards before coming down. I decided not to bother about him for the time being, and just as well, for shortly afterwards I spotted a single drake approaching, again inshore of me. This bird pitched in the burn rather a long shot away, and I was just wondering what to do about it when out of the tail of my eye I caught sight of six more mallard approaching on the same course. Two of the newcomers, both drakes, were flying very close together and as they crossed my front at about 35 yards, I dropped them both with one shot, again killing a duck with the left barrel. One of the drakes was only winged and gave me a hard chase across the seaweed-covered stones before I finally caught up with it just short of the tide's edge.

Just before the tide reached the butt, a single mallard came straight at me, travelling at a tremendous rate with the wind behind it, so I stood right up in an attempt to get it to climb and so slow it up a bit. This manoeuvre succeeded, and although I apparently missed it with my first shot, my second had it " dead in the air "another fine drake—and a really first-class effort which pleased me no end. Shortly after this, the tide washed me out of the butt, so I packed up and set out to look for the duck I had shot earlier and which had come down behind me. Because of the gloom I had been unable to mark this bird very well, and a duck lying among seaweed and stones takes a lot of finding. However, after a long and careful search I finally picked it up stone-dead another drake. This brought the bag up to eight . . . five drakes and three ducks, which wasn't too bad for nine cartridges fired !

I thought of waiting until after high water to try for some golden plover, but changed my mind and decided to go home, have some breakfast, and then go out to the merse edge in the hope of a tide-flight developing. This, in fact, is what I did do, and it very nearly paid off. A tide-flight did develop and a good number of wigeon were on the move. Several lots actually pitched on the merse, and if the creeks had not been half full of water I would have attempted to stalk some of them. But it was out of the question, so I just had to sit tight and hope for the best. One lot of about 40 flew round for quite a while, time and again passing just out of shot, and eventually pitching less than 100 yards away. Unfortunately I couldn't get a yard closer, so there was nothing I could do about them. Shortly afterwards I decided to move them, as they were doing me little good. Other small packs of wigeon which might have given me a chance, were inevitably drawn to them. Perhaps I had used up all my luck at morning flight, for even after this, several parties of wigeon, up to about 30 in number, passed me just out of range. I only had two shots at a little bunch of five but managed to bag a couple.

On the way home I lost a first-class chance at five mallard while crossing a large and deep creek. In the interests of safety I had unloaded my gun and was ploughing through the soft mud in the creek bottom, when these birds sailed over so close I could have seen the white in their eyes if they had had any! All in all, and despite two changes of wet clothing, quite an interesting and exciting day.

Dark Passage

TO punt-gunners, old and new, WAGBIs successful defence of this branch of wildfowling against a determined attempt to have it banned, must have come as a great relief. And not only to punt-gunners but to a great many other people as well, for on the premise that logically, if you ban one form of shooting you ban the lot, it may well be that this victory prevented the insertion of the " thin end of the wedge " into the entire sport of shooting. Even if this view is over-pessimistic it has at least saved, for the time being, a form of sport considered by its devotees to be second to none, for while it is true that salt-water punting is actively pursued by a comparatively small number of enthusiasts, it is equally true that it is one of the most exciting as well as exacting forms of shooting left to us.

Three times the punt filled to the brim . . . Ferryman

It is, of course, a highly specialised business, and a lot of experience is necessary before there is much chance of success. It can also be arduous in the extreme, and somewhat dangerous, but few, if any, puntsmen are genuine masochists, and the discomforts and risks are accepted rather than welcomed. Having had my share of the thrills and spills of this sport, it is good to know that it is still available to those who are prepared to tackle its inherent difficulties and frustrations, and these certainly exist, as may be gathered from the following experience which occurred during the lengthy period in which I served my punting apprenticeship.

Having heard of a sizeable company of wigeon which were said to be frequenting a certain tidal reach of the river about 5 miles upstream from our mooring creek, I determined to try for a shot at them on the following Saturday afternoon, this being the only free time I had available. The date was far from ideal ; high tide did not occur until about two hours after dark, and since I would be obliged to wait until the ebb had set in before setting course for home, this would mean a long and tricky passage down-river in the dark. I was well aware of the risk involved as this section of river which flows between high mud banks, is obstructed in a number of places by stone jetties which have been constructed to prevent erosion. These jetties, apart from being a danger in themselves, create powerful eddies which I knew from experience were capable of spinning the punt round like a top. In addition, and particularly when the wind was opposed to the tide, the turbulence caused was very considerable, and in a punt with its low freeboard, great care must be taken. However, I had often navigated this part of the river in daylight and felt quite capable of tackling it in the dark. All I needed was a reasonably clear night and a fair wind home.

Saturday opened bright and sunny, and almost windless, but by the time I reached home, shortly after noon, a stiff breeze was blowing from the sou'-west and an ominous haze had spread across the sky. I was somewhat uneasy as I prepared the punt for launching, but having looked forward to this outing, almost to the total exclusion of everything else, I was very reluctant to cancel or even amend it. As soon, therefore, as there was sufficient tide in the creek I slid the punt into the water and set off. Once out in the main river I stopped to load the puntgun, a handy weapon loaned to me by my old friend Adam. A breech-loader with a drop-down action, it fired around 8 ounces of shot, hand-loaded into steel cases, and was as easy to load as a 12-bore. There being nothing of interest in sight I stepped the mast, hoisted a little lug-sail, and running before the wind and tide, set off up-river at a fair clip.

Since there was a possibility of encountering duck in almost any part of the river, I kept a sharp lookout ahead, but except for the odd mallard and one small bunch of teal, I saw nothing of interest. On arriving at my destination, a wide stretch of river with a long mud bank in the middle, I spied the area carefully, but to my great disappointment all the duck I could spot were four mallard sitting on a clay hummock at the foot of a steep clay bank. Convinced that the reported wigeon were nowhere about, I decided to try for a shot at the mallard with my single barrel 12-bore cripple-stopper. Two of these birds were sitting very close together, and I thought I might manage to shoot them both with one shot. Loading the 12-bore, I laid it alongside the puntgun, and with the setting-pole in my left hand quietly set the punt towards the mallard.

At about 45 yards they became highly suspicious and stood up with their necks at full stretch. Holding the gun with one hand by the pistol grip and steadying the punt with the other, I fired just over the heads of the pair I had marked. The shot caught them in the middle of their jump and they both dropped back into the water. Before I had time to congratulate myself on the success of my shot there was a roar of wings and about 200 wigeon took off from the top of the high bank ahead of me where a later inspection showed they had been feeding on the grass. At first I thought all was not lost, for they pitched momentarily in the river ahead of me, but almost immediately changed their minds, and flying down past me disappeared from, view.

Bitterly disappointed I sat cursing my ill-judgment. " Why, oh why, hadn't I waited quietly for a time just in case they were up on the grass somewhere?" " Sooner or later they would have flown down into the river, for this was the way of wigeon in open weather—always on the *qui vive* and ready to flip down on to the water on the slightest suspicion." Oh well, I would know better next time ! Paddling inshore I picked up the two mallard, and after examining the area in which the wigeon had been feeding, re-embarked and rowed up to the mud bank ahead of me. This was a famous place for waders, and I had hopes of bagging a few golden plover with the 12-bore. Already I could see large numbers of plover, both green and golden, circling the fields in the distance, and knew that before dark some of them would almost certainly come down to roost on the mud.

Sure enough a good flight developed and by the time it was dark I had 17 golden plover and three curlew down, most of which were still lying out on the mud, which was much too soft to walk upon. This brisk session had kept my mind off the weather, which by now was far from good. Towards dusk the wind had freshened to gale force, and as darkness fell, it began to rain heavily. It was obviously going to be a very dirty night!

As soon as the punt would float over the mud, I collected the slain, and despite the fact that the tide was still against me, I decided to make what progress I could down-river before it was too dark to see what lay ahead. In preparation for what I knew would be a rough passage, I slipped the breeching rope off the punt-gun's trunnions, pulled the gun inboard and laid it flat on the cockpit floor. Leaving out the oars and a long setting-pole, I pushed everything else that would float under the gun-deck, wedging it in place with the ammunition box. The kill was, as usual, packed up each side of the cockpit, this being the only space available. Hanging my precious binoculars round my neck, I picked up the long pole, and standing upright to get as much purchase as possible, set out for home.

With wind and tide against me, progress was very slow, but by the time the latter turned in my favour I had covered a couple of hard-earned miles. It was now almost pitch dark and, apart from a few distant lights, I could see only the white wave tops as they raced towards me. I had now reached the area of the stone jetties, so, abandoning the setting-pole, I got out the oars and rowed well out into the river in order to avoid these dangerous obstacles. For a time all went fairly well and, with the aid of the strong ebb tide, I made reasonable progress. Admittedly I did run ashore once or twice, and later on narrowly escaped collision with a jetty, but not until I reached a narrow part of the river where two of these stood directly opposite each other, did I run into really serious trouble.

The wind funnelling through the gap was creating a rough and confused sea which, had I been able to see it, would probably have deterred me from even attempting to pass through in my little punt. However, guided almost entirely by sound, I succeeded in getting through, but in doing so the punt shipped an alarming amount of water. These being the last of the jetties, I edged across to my "own" bank and after bailing most of the water out of the punt, set out on " the last mile home." The river below this point quickly widens out into a considerable estuary, and judging from the roar of the sea I knew further troubles lay ahead for me.

Determined not to venture out into deep water where a capsize would have meant the loss of all my gear, if not my life, I poled along through the breaking seas down the merse edge. Three times the punt filled to the brim, twice I succeeded in bailing her out, standing waist-deep in the water, and holding her head-on to the waves with one hand and bailing with the other. Each time my stock of plover grew less as the bailer scooped up the little birds which were floating around in the cockpit. On the third occasion, when the punt was swamped by a great comber only a few hundred yards from the mooring creek, I was so exhausted that the best I could do was to tow the punt ashore through the surf, anchor it securely, and stagger homeward across the merse carrying my most precious items of equipment, and the pair of mallard —all I was able to rescue.

. . . the geese approached just to one side of me. . . .

THE ONES THAT GOT AWAY

ALTHOUGH I suppose it must be a fairly common occurrence for shot birds to recover and fly off before they are retrieved—indeed I have seen this happen on a good number of occasions— it must be quite unusual for one to do so after it has been picked up, apparently dead, and placed with the slain for well over an hour. This is precisely what happened one wet and windy day in the winter of 1957 when my son and I were " tide fighting " wigeon from a creek on the merse edge.

We had gone out at first light, hoping for a shot at the geese, but although we had seen and heard several skeins, none had come near us. Now it was broad daylight and the tide was beginning to flow up the estuary, but since it was a period of neap tides, making it perfectly safe to remain out on the merse until high water, we decided to wait in the hope of a tide flight developing. The rain, which had been threatening all morning, came on soon after daylight and gradually developed into a steady downpour. However, the wigeon had started moving, so we determined to stick it out. Moving out towards the merse edge we took up positions about a gunshot apart in the same creek, and were fortunate enough to get several parties of wigeon which were " cutting the corner " on their way up the estuary.

Although our shooting was none too good we eventually had seven wigeon down, all of which were picked up by my son, and our gamebag being in use as a cover for our binoculars and cartridge bags, these birds were placed in a heap on a grassy ledge close to his hide. Eventually, after a long lull in the shooting, a skein of pinkfeet appeared in the distance, and, in attempting to replace his No. 5 shot cartridges with BB's, the extractor of my son's gun pulled past the head of a badly swollen cartridge, putting him completely out of action. The pink-feet, in fact, came right over us, but being too high were allowed to pass unsaluted. Being informed of the trouble, I laid down my gun on the merse grass and waded up the creek to help to clear the jam. With the tip of a penknife blade we

Ferryman recalls three occasions when the birds were down for the count but took off again

were able to turn the set-screw holding the extractor in place and were in the act of removing the latter when my son noticed one of the wigeon, an adult drake, standing upright beside the little heap of duck. Since we were fully occupied and there appeared little likelihood of the wigeon escaping, we took no action for the moment. A few seconds later, to our complete astonishment, it took off, and flying strongly out over the mud, disappeared into the distance, apparently none the worse !

Not the least surprising thing about this incident was the fact that this was the second time something similar had happened when I had been shooting from this very creek, although it had happened a long time previously. I was about 18 years old at the time, and had gone out alone for morning flight armed with my treasured " Knoxall " 12-bore single-barrel gun. No geese had come my way at first light, but several companies of wigeon had, out of which I had managed to knock down five. Even after it was broad daylight a number of wigeon were still on the move, and since there were signs that some of them would most probably fly up on to the merse to feed on the sweet grass, I decided to set up my dead birds as decoys. With sheets of newspaper, carried in my gamebag especially for the purpose, I carefully cleaned each bird and thrust a straight piece of wire under each bird's " chin " ; they were now ready to set up.

As so often happens on these occasions, I was in the act of climbing out of the creek, when a single wigeon appeared from nowhere. Snatching up the gun I fired as it swung away towards the river and it fell with a thump on the mud, a short distance out from the merse edge. After reloading, I climbed out of the creek to retrieve this bird which was lying on its back and apparently stone-dead. Picking it up by the head, I was just about to return to my stance when I heard a goose call, and looking in the direction of the sound, saw a little line of greylags approaching, and at no great distance. To regain the creek without attracting the attention of the geese was well nigh impossible, so, dropping the wigeon on to the mud, I slid quietly into the only cover available, a tiny mud gutter, little more than a foot deep. Never being one to worry overmuch about mud when there were geese about, I lay flat on my back, my feet towards the oncoming geese, holding the gun on my chest with my elbows, and covering my face with my hands. Peering though my muddy fingers,

I watched with bated breath as the geese approached, just to one side of me, and wished fervently that I had put a BB cartridge into the chamber instead of a No. 5. When I judged the right moment had come I sat up, not without difficulty, and fired at the last goose in the line ; it crumpled up and dropped towards me like a stone.

The kick of the gun (for the old Knoxall was a great one to kick, being rather light in the barrel) upset my rather insecure balance and I toppled over sideways and backwards. Out of the tail of my eye I glimpsed the goose coming straight at my face and only just managed to flick my head to the side as it thumped into the mud by my right ear, the tip of one wing striking me a stinging blow on the cheek. Rising to my feet I picked up the goose and turned to collect the wigeon which I had dropped a few feet away—it was nowhere to be seen ! Looking at the spot where it had lain, I could see by the prints in the soft mud that it had evidently recovered, walked a few yards, and then, probably when I fired at the goose, flown off unnoticed.

The third and only other successful " getaway " in which I was personally involved, occurred when out punting with my friend Bob. We had had a reasonably successful shot with the puntgun at a mixed bunch of wigeon and teal, and after a hectic cripple-chase in very rough water, had rowed inshore to bail the punt and get things organised. As always, following a shot, the floor of the punt was littered with gear and dead duck, tossed in any old way, and our first job on running ashore was to shake the water out of each duck's feathers and arrange them neatly on the foredeck to dry. Having done this, we removed the short section of the floorboards aft and with bailer and sponge proceeded to get the punt clean and dry. In the middle of this operation one of the " dead " teal suddenly stood up, and before we could make a move to stop it, it jumped into the air and flew off.

With an exclamation Bob dropped the bailer and grabbed the nearest cripple-stopper, a single 12-bore, which was lying handy across the short stern deck. The teal was already about 35 yards away and going strong. Bob cocked the hammer, swung, and pulled. Click ! With a laugh he turned to me. " Well, I'm hanged ! I forgot that I never bothered to reload after that last shot." Picking up the binoculars, I watched the teal until it was little more than a tiny speck in the distance. " Oh, well," said Bob, " I reckon that little chap deserves to get away after all that." I agreed most heartily.

ONE of the great joys of punting is that, given reasonable weather, each and every outing can be exciting and enjoyable, even the inevitable " blank days " during which not a single shot is fired. Indeed, in retrospect, some of my most pleasant memories fall into this category, usually for widely differing reasons. One such outing which I always recall with a smile concerned myself only.

Out in my single punt on a fine calm morning, I found it quite impossible to get within range of the wigeon which were my main quarry. Time and again I set the punt to likely looking companies, but always they jumped before I was close enough for a shot. No matter how carefully I approached, their necks would stretch in alarm, and with a roar of wings they were up and away.

Being of a persevering nature I continued to try and ended up, still duckless, several miles down the estuary where the main channel reaches the open sea ; this is a marvellous place of mighty sandbanks, firm enough to support a bus. Having some time to spend before the flowing tide would enable me to start the return cruise up the estuary, I took the opportunity of eating my sandwiches, and then went ashore

Ferryman enjoys a blank day

to stretch my legs and take a look through the glasses. Away to seaward, gently rising and falling on the glassy swells, were several black rafts of duck, but nowhere could I see anything remotely accessible to the punt, even in these calm conditions. The best remaining chance was when the tide started to flow and some of these duck would fly up the estuary ahead of me, pitching in or alongside the main river channel. This was quite a normal occurrence, and since I would then have the sun behind me, there was a good chance that I might yet pull off a shot.

In a short time the flood set in and not long afterwards, several companies of wigeon flew up and disappeared into the shimmering haze of the estuary. Waiting until the tide was moving strongly in my favour I set off, and after covering a mile or so, paused to spy the situation up ahead of me. Almost at the limit of visibility I could see what looked like a sizeable party of duck sitting on top of a high sandbank on the opposite side of the channel, so, rowing across, I set out to try for a shot. Lying down while still a long way from the duck, I made good progress and eventually got close enough to see with the naked eye that the company consisted of about 150 wigeon, most of them apparently asleep in the sunshine. Approaching as I was, right out of the eye of the sun, things looked good for a shot, but there was a snag—a big one! The edge of the sand-cum-mudbank upon which the duck were sitting had been eroded by the current, which had created a cut-bank several feet high. Once I was within range of the duck it would be quite impossible to shoot over this until the tide had lifted the punt about a couple of feet. There was nothing else for it—I would just have to wait!

Running in under the cut-bank I stopped the punt when I thought I was about the right distance from the wigeon, and cautiously raising my head, peeped over the edge. They were there all right, basking in the sunshine, the crowns of the drakes' heads gleaming like newly-minted gold. Estimating that it might be 20 minutes or so before the punt had floated high enough, I quietly slipped the grapnel overboard, lay down, face upward, in the bottom of the punt, closed my eyes against the glare, and settled down to wait. A long time later I awoke, somewhat puzzled to begin with, and then, remembering where I was, I raised my head and looked over the coaming of the punt. Blue water ruffled by a slight breeze stretched for miles in every direction, while the punt rocked gently at her anchor; of the wigeon there was not a sign! I sometimes wonder how they reacted when the punt floated up into full view, almost on their doorstep, so to speak. I shall never know!

In April 1968 a count of the wild whooper swans present in the estuary resulted in a total of 64. This is the greatest number so far noted, although totals not far short of this have been present from time to time for the past few years. During their stay with us these birds live almost exclusively on the land of one farmer whose fields border the river at the head of the estuary, grazing like sheep, nearly always in the same field. They make short flights daily to the nearby river to wash and preen, and occasionally make longer flights down the estuary, invariably returning to their chosen feeding grounds. Not unnaturally, the owner of the fields is rather annoyed at the presence of these birds, which eat an astonishing amount of grass and puddle large areas with their huge feet. From time to time he has made efforts to drive them away, but as soon as the coast is clear they are back again in their favourite field or a neighbouring one.

In my younger days, whoopers were rather irregular visitors to our estuary and were usually to be found only in family parties. Occasionally we encountered small herds when out punting, but we never attempted to approach them until my late brother, Jack, acquired a copy of the Diaries of Colonel Peter Hawker. From this well-loved volume we learned that the *piece de résistance* of this redoubtable gentleman's wildfowling expeditions was the shooting of wild swans. From Hawker's accounts it appears certain that in his day, probably due to excessive persecution, these birds were almost unapproachable. My brother and I, in discussing this, decided that at the first suitable opportunity when out punting we would attempt to get as close as possible to some whoopers to see what changes time, and protection, had wrought.

One day, homeward bound from a punting expedition, the ideal opportunity presented itself — seven whoopers drifting slowly along in shallow water, and apparently fast asleep. We knew for certain they were whoopers long before we were anywhere near them, for earlier in the day we had both seen and heard them arrive. Taking no chances of their waking up and having a look around, we lay down while still a long way off, and, aided by a swiftly flowing tide, set the punt towards them. Soon we were within Hawker's "pistol ball" range, then within "mould shot" range, and still not a sign of movement from the swans. Quickly the range shortened as Jack gently eased the punt forward, pushing on the muddy bottom with a short setting-pole and making not the least whisper of sound. Even although we had no intention of shooting at these birds, the old excitement was there and I felt my heartbeats quicken as they always do towards the end of a stalk. Closer and closer we drew — now the punt's bow was almost abreast of the nearest swan which was less than 15 feet away, and peeping over the edge of the coaming we could see that the herd consisted of four old and three immature birds. The long necks were laid across the backs, the heads being completely hidden in the wing feathers.

Fascinated and somewhat awed by our close proximity to these wild and wonderful creatures, we gazed at them as the punt drifted quietly along. Suddenly, as though warned of our presence by some sixth sense, one long neck shot stiffly erect, and the wedge-shaped head turned in our direction. A single glance from the beady eyes, a single warning note and the entire herd was on the move, their legs paddling like mad and the spray flying as their great wings beat the surface of the water in a frantic endeavour to get airborne in the shortest possible time.

As we sat up and watched them fly off towards the head of the bay, trumpeting and hoo-hoo-hooing with indignation we wondered what the old Colonel would have thought of a pair of puntsmen who watched wild swans at point-blank range! It may be of interest to note that on several subsequent occasions we set the punt to parties of very wide-awake whoopers and usually got to within fair range without much difficulty.

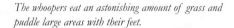
The whoopers eat an astonishing amount of grass and puddle large areas with their feet.

John Marchington

PRENTICE FOWLER

Ferryman answers a simple question

NOT very long ago I was asked a perfectly simple and straightforward question, "What made you take up wildfowling?" Now having been a fowler almost all my life, this should have been an easy question to answer and, indeed, my first reaction was to say, " Well, what could be more natural?" After all I have lived most of my life within sight and sound of an important winter duck and goose haunt, right on the spot so to speak; the incentive was always there. But on second thoughts it occurred to me that it wasn't as simple as all that. Exactly the same conditions applied to all my schoolfellows, yet very few had taken up wildfowling as a sport, and only a small number had shown more than a passing interest in the wildfowl themselves. Even the clamouring skeins of greylags, which sent me into ecstasies of excitement as they flew over the playground of our village school, aroused only mild and transient interest in most of my schoolfellows.

No ! There must be more to it than that ! Even my early interest in guns and in shooting wasn't so easy to define, and certainly did not stem from any encouragement received from adult members of my family. My father scarcely knew one end of a gun from the other, being almost totally absorbed by his beloved hobby of music. Not that he went out of his way to discourage me but I think it took him a long time to understand my passionate interest in guns, and the art of wildfowling. To begin with, as a young schoolboy, I satisfied my urge to participate simply by watching the activities of the local and visiting fowlers, and listening avidly to any snatches of conversation I could overhear. This had to be done with considerable circumspection, as men in those days did not readily tolerate small boys; there was always the risk of receiving a tap on the behind with the toe of a seaboot if one got too nosey !

Later, things became easier when I succeeded in gaining the entrée to the " Fishhouse," in the cosy back-room of which foregathered the local fisherman and fowlers, and where, sooner or later, one was sure to meet visiting wildfowlers of any importance. Being allowed into this marvellous room was, for a schoolboy, a privilege difficult to imagine nowadays, and was only possible because of a friendship I had struck up with the owner, who, despite my extreme youth, must have recognised in me a kindred spirit.

Evenings at the Fishhouse

Adam was a salmon fisherman by profession, and an expert puntsman by choice. He was also, amongst other things, a naturalist and antiquarian of note. At this period he and his friend, the " Major," were the top punting team in our district, operating over a wide area in a punt of their own construction, which they towed from place to place on a trailer. The Fishhouse was their headquarters, and at every opportunity I would waylay them on their return, helping perhaps to unload the duck (usually wigeon), rub them clean and hang them on the rafters to dry. In the evening, the fire would be lit in the back-room and fed with logs of sawn-up driftwood or broken salmon net stakes. If the flames died down, pieces of tarry net were added, and soon the fire would be blazing merrily again. Oh ! the delightful smell of that room! A smell compounded of gun oil, tar and tobacco—it remains with me to this day !

On a typical evening, ranged round the fire on home-made stools, would be a small group of fisherman-fowlers, with perhaps one or two others who simply liked the atmosphere of the place. Apart from the firelight, only one or two candles in old-fashioned candlesticks supplied the light, even when the Major was loading puntgun cartridges at his bench in the corner of the room. In the gunrack would be the " cripple-stoppers," including the Major's unusual side-lever double 12-bore, and if they had been used that day I would take them down and clean and oil them with meticulous care, listening all the time to the conversation, which was usually about the doings of the day, or fowling in general.

In this august company I never spoke unless I was directly addressed, and although I made myself useful I also made myself as inconspicuous as possible. Nevertheless, I soon made a niche for myself, and by the end of the first winter was accepted as a " regular " and was invited occasionally to contribute to the conversation. . ... What a wonderful winter that was! The only fly in the ointment being the regular 9 p.m. curfew imposed on me by my parents. However, our house was only about a couple of minutes " run " from the Fishhouse, so I was able to remain almost literally to the last minute. During the following winter my parents agreed to let me go out occasionally with one or other of the local wildfowlers, and during my very first moonlight shoot I had the never-to-beforgotten thrill of seeing my first greylag geese shot and, to add to the thrill, was the knowledge that if I had not been there, it is most unlikely that these birds would have been bagged at all !

A line of blobs

Young Will was the son of one of the local fisherman, and the Major, knowing how keen I was, offered to loan Will his single 8-bore provided he would take me with him on his next moonlight foray. Will was nothing loth, and so began an association which lasted until he emigrated to the U.S.A. several years later.

The night chosen for our foray was two nights before the full moon, and at least an hour before we were due to leave, I knocked on Will's door, was admitted and sat by the fire feeling very self-conscious, dressed as I was in my oldest and heaviest clothing. In due course Will made a few leisurely preparations, and at long last we were off ! Every moment of that outing was a thrill, and as we stood side by side in a creek from which I have shot hundreds of times since, I shivered more from excitement than from cold. The night was almost completely cloudless, which was a bad thing Will announced, since it would make the birds very difficult to see. However the strong north-easterly wind was in our favour and would tend to keep the geese low if, and when, they came off the sands, although there appeared to be grave doubts about this happening.

Time went past during which Will smoked pipe after pipe of tobacco, and held desultory conversation with me, cracking jokes (he was a great joker) mainly about the unlikelihood of our seeing, much less shooting any geese that night. The pipe once again having gone out, he was in the act of relighting it, bent double in the creek-bottom to keep out of the wind, when I spotted a line of dark blobs in the sky, approaching silently. Uncertain of what they were I prodded Will with my finger, pointed to the blobs and said, "What are those." Will straightened up and was instantly galvanised into action. " Geese," he hissed, dropping his pipe on the grass in a shower of sparks, and seizing the 8-bore. The line of blobs was now passing on our right at about 40 yards range. I watched them, scarcely daring to breathe. The 8-bore crashed, the geese gabbled in alarm, and two of the blobs detached themselves from the line, dropping straight down on to the merse grass. " Get them," cried Will. In a trice I was out of the creek, and a minute later returned carrying the first geese I had ever handled. I fondled each in turn, scarcely believing they could be real. I tucked my small cold hands into the warm feathers beneath their wings, and longed for the day when I should have a gun of my own, and bag beauties like these.

*   *   *   *

Here then in the magic of these moments was confirmed one already born to be a fowler. The answer to the question was really quite simple after all.

BUTTERFLY DAY

THE morning was calm and still, not the faintest breath of wind ruffled the surface of the water, as my brother Jack and I rowed steadily down the shining moon path towards the mouth of the tributary.

The squeak of the rowlocks, even the sound of the long double punt cutting through the water, sounded unnaturally loud in the utter silence . . . it was a perfect morning . . . but not for wild-fowling! However, there was always the chance that a breeze would spring up at daybreak and even if it did not, we were quite undismayed, for we knew we would enjoy our outing whatever the outcome. Half a mile or so above the tributary we loaded the puntgun, my brother lay down in the firing position, while I, kneeling in the stern, pushed the punt along through the shallow water with the setting pole. As we got closer the glasses revealed about 30 or 40 duck swimming in the mouth of the little river, which, from their movements, we concluded to be the resident flock of shoveller. This proved to be the case and at about 120 yards range they rose with a great clattering of wings, and vanished down the main river. For a few minutes we lay-to in the mouth of the tributary, spying with the glasses and listening for the sound of duck or geese, but apart from the distant quacking of a few mallard we heard nothing of interest. After a short council of war we decided that in these calm conditions, our best chance lay in pushing up the tributary and lying in the shadow of the high clay banks from which position we could drop rapidly downstream on any duck which might pitch in, or beside the river below us.

All the omens were wrong, writes Ferryman, but there was a chance . . .

This was a plan we had used successfully many times previously, so getting out our long setting poles we proceeded to put it into action.

Upon reaching our objective, we anchored the punt and sat listening to the rapidly awakening bird life around us. As the eastern sky turned paler and paler grey, a babble of sound arose; oystercatchers in their hundreds piped shrilly, curlew called incessantly, gulls gossiped to each other as great rafts left their roosts on the sands and swept inland to feed. Up on the high sands a gaggle of pinkfeet awoke and began to gabble and quarrel amongst themselves. Suddenly they were silent for a few moments and then, with a great outcry, swept into the air and followed the gulls inland. We listened to their voices receding into the distance as they crossed a wide stretch of merseland, but no shot greeted them . . . no doubt these crafty birds had climbed high above the reach of any gun.

In our immediate vicinity things were beginning to liven up; several little parties of duck, both teal and wigeon, whistled past us as we sat quietly in the shadow of the high clay bank. Some of these were within range of our 12-bores but we let them go, not wishing to disturb the area, as a shot in these conditions would be heard for miles. Eventually a dark mass of birds appeared near the mouth of the tributary, flew upstream for a short distance and pitched with a mighty splash in the little river . . . wigeon!

We could distinctly hear the whistling of the cocks and the purring and growling of the hens. In a minute or two they were all ashore or standing in the shallows, splashing and beating the water with their wings as they busily washed and preened. Since it was now almost daylight we decided to try for a shot without delay, and in a few moments the punt was under way and shooting swiftly towards the duck. For a minute or so all went well, and then suddenly they were all in the air! What put them up we will never know . . . it certainly couldn't have been us, for we were still a long way from them, and in any case they would have gone off in the opposite direction . . . but here they were, only a few yards above the water and flying straight up river towards us! Jack, who was at the gun whispered urgently over his shoulder, "What do you want me to do." "Cock the gun," I replied, "and if they keep coming the way they're doing at the moment, shoot the instant they're within range." Swiftly the distance between the punt and the coming duck closed. Lying flat in the stern with only one arm over the side, my hand and forearm in the water to make the minimum of movement visible to the duck, I strove with the setting pole to hold the punt on a dead straight line. Suddenly, without warning, the great gun boomed, the thunder of the shot rolling across the bay and echoing back from the neighbouring hills. Seconds later the water all round the racing punt erupted in a series of splashes as dead wigeon came hurtling through the pall of gunsmoke, several missing the cockpit by inches, and one which struck the gun deck, narrowly missing Jack's face. Some of the duck actually splashed down *behind* the punt, so rapid had our "collision courses" been. Following a hectic pick-up in the fast water and a short cripple chase, we found ourselves once again out in the main river. After cleaning and reloading the puntgun, we tidied up the punt and stowed the wigeon away, counting them as we did so. We had shot 21 wigeon with our head on flying shot! Although there seemed little likelihood of our getting another shot, we decided to cruise on down the main river as far as the open sea, just for the pleasure of it.

Later, moored alongside a great golden sandbank, we sat in brilliant sunshine drinking our tea and eating our sandwiches as we awaited the turn of the tide. Already we had stripped off much of our heavy clothing, which had made us uncomfortably warm. Something resembling a heat haze shimmered over the sandbanks behind us, reminding us of a day in June. It was, we agreed, definitely not a day for wildfowling, and yet . . . we smiled at each other and looked at our 21 wigeon. Soon the tide began to flow, and since it was still glassy calm we got out the oars and set off homeward, not hurrying, just rowing along at a leisurely pace, enjoying each others company and the perfection of the day. Ahead of us in the distance we could see several black patches that looked as though they might be duck, but we entertained little hope of getting another shot. However the sun was now behind us so there was just a chance that by approaching up the sun path we *might* get close enough, always providing we could find some duck in the right place and that they would be in sufficient numbers to justify the attempt.

Eventually, about a mile ahead, we spotted a fair sized company of wigeon, scattered, but not too badly scattered, on the water. After studying them for some time through the glasses, I thought that there might be a possible chance, and asked Jack the minimum number he considered we should shoot for. "A dozen," he replied without hesitation. "Right," said I, "get me within range of that lot and I'll shoot you a dozen!"

Without further ado we commenced the stalk, the punt moving along quite easily, helped by the flowing tide. To begin with Jack pushed along vigorously and although the duck were also drifting slowly along on the tide, we quickly began to overtake them. As we got nearer we took great care to keep the punt, as far as this was possible, right in the eye of the sun. Jack also slowed up his rate of progress to avoid leaving too obvious a wake in the glassy water. Slowly the range shortened; the punt was now little more than drifting along, so careful was Jack's approach. Peeping past the side of the gun I watched the duck slowly change from a nondescript colour to clearly defined hens and cocks ; we were within range and I was more than a little surprised. Raising my head carefully I took rapid stock of the situation. We were still at long range, nowhere were the duck very thick, but somewhat to our left a group of about a score looked like the best chance.

"Left, Jack, left!" I whispered urgently, and the punt's bow moved slowly round in the desired direction. Suddenly the duck started swimming rapidly away from us, their necks stretched to full length . . . they were about to go. Pushing down on the gunstock with my left hand, I pulled the lanyard at the precise instant the duck leapt from the water. Again the boom of the big gun rolled out across the bay, and a pall of smoke lay across our bows making it impossible to see the results of our shot. Quickly Jack sat up and pushed the punt through the gunsmoke, while I unlimbered and loaded a cripple stopper. I had more than fulfilled my promise; 13 duck were down, three of which were still alive, and quickly given a *coup-de-grâce*. Paddling around we scooped them up one after the other with the landing-net.

As we rowed in bright sunshine past the Old Quay, where road and river run parallel for a short distance, a car pulled up and a large bearded figure, now a well-known film actor, emerged. "Ahoy!" he bellowed, "what the devil are you doing out punting on a day like this?" "It's only fit for catching butterflies!" By way of an answer we each laid down our oar, and reaching into the cockpit held up a double handful of wigeon. "Well I'm damned," said he, "I wouldn't have believed it!"

Tales from the Fishouse Inn

Two anecdotes from Ferryman

Among the many tales related to me as we sat round the fire in the cosy back room of the Fishouse, 'way back in the 1920s, two stand out clearly in my memory : the story of Willie's goose, and of the shooting match. The first of these anecdotes was related to me by the Major on the evening after it occurred, the other was told and retold, having occurred a year or two earlier, although the participants were well known to me.

The Major and Adam had planned a dawn attack on the geese which often came to drink and wash in the tidal part of a large burn which flowed into a bay some 20 miles away. In preparation for this, and accompanied by Adam's brother Willie, who had volunteered to assist, they set out in the early afternoon with the punt on its trailer, intending to launch it and then return to base for the night. Not far short of their destination they spotted a party of greylags feeding in a field, and stopped the car to have a look at them through the glasses. The field was as flat as a board, but a deep ditch ran along one side, and although the nearest geese appeared to be about 70 or 80 yards from the ditch, Willie declared his intention of stalking them. The Major immediately offered to lay a bet that he couldn't possibly shoot a goose at that range, particularly since the only cartridges available were loaded with No. 6 shot, but Willie wasn't to be put off, and taking one of the cripple-stoppers out of the car, slipped into the ditch at the roadside and commenced the stalk.

Eventually the watching pair noticed that the geese had stopped feeding and were standing on the alert, and almost at the same moment Willie's head emerged from the creek. As the geese jumped, the thump of two shots rang out across the field, and to the astonishment of the onlookers, one goose flopped back on to the ground, its wings beating the grass as it vainly tried to become airborne. Climbing out of the ditch Willie made a gesture of triumph in the direction of the car and then hurried across to secure his prize. Seizing the goose by the neck he took a step towards the road, and then suddenly halted; his short-lived triumph was at an end, he hadn't shot the goose after all, it was caught by the leg in a rabit snare! Subsequent investigations showed that the field was liberally set with snares, a professional rabbit-catcher being at work on the farm at the time. Knowing that every move was being watched, Willie didn't bother claiming to have shot the goose, but he did claim to have won the bet, since he hadn't returned empty-handed.

Among the many habitués of the Fishouse at the time of the following event, was a certain Sandy K—, a worthy, who combined the business of butcher and small farmer. A great practical joker, Sandy never missed a chance of pulling the leg of any less imaginative member of the group who gave him an opening. One day, when deliberately boasting about his prowess with a gun, he so incensed an old and somewhat short-tempered fisherman, also named Sandy, that the latter offered to bet half-a-crown (a tidy sum in those days), that the butcher couldn't " hit his bonnet " if he threw it in the air. The fisherman was somewhat taken aback when the butcher promptly accepted this bet, and would have called it off had he dared. However, without loss of face there was no way out, and since it was early in the season, and still broad daylight, it was decided that the matter should be settled then and there.

The fisherman, with a howl of fury, gaped at his desecrated headgear

Adam, being the occupier of the place, was naturally appointed Master of Ceremonies, and offered to supply a gun and a couple of cartridges. The money having been handed over to his brother Willie, who was to act as stake-holder, Adam, gun in hand, led the way to the nearby slaughter house, in the vicinity of which the " shoot " was to take place. A few minutes later, having arrived at the scene of action, the final details were settled and the protagonists took up their stands. The fisherman, cap in hand, stood behind the gable end of the little building, with the butcher standing a short distance back from the opposite end. At a signal from Adam, the cap, a padded seaman's affair with a stem, known locally as a "cheese-cutter," was to be tossed upward and forward, and the butcher was to shoot at will.

"Are you ready K— ? " called Adam. " Aye," replied the butcher, cocking both barrels of the gun.

"Are you ready H— ? " called Adam again.

"Lang ago," replied the fisherman irritably.

"Right! " shouted Adam, " Ready! throw ! "

An instant later the cap sailed into view and the onlookers watched intently as the gun barrels swung upwards to intercept it in mid-flight. Up it curved, then downwards, and as it bounced onto the grass, not very far from where he was standing, the butcher let drive with both barrels! This action took everyone by surprise, not least the fisherman, who with a howl of fury, shot out of his hideout and gaped at his desecrated headgear. Streaks of white festooned the grass where the pellets had torn the cottonwool stuffing out of the cap, and it was apparent that the butcher had scored a couple of bullseyes!

Yelling with laughter, he thrust the gun into Willie's hands and beat a hasty retreat, hotly pursued by the furious fisherman. The latter, having been restrained by some of the onlookers, was somewhat mollified when Adam awarded him the bet, having declared the butcher disqualified for unfair tactics. Although it was suggested that the fisherman might use the butcher's half-crown to buy himself a new cap, which it would well have done, it was noted that he did nothing of the sort, but continued to wear the shot-up old " cheese-cutter," crudely repaired, for the rest of his life.

GOLDIES GALORE

The sport was fast and furious, writes Ferryman

EACH time my friend Pat and his guests came up to Scotland for a winter holiday, a day or two at the golden plover has always been planned. Although, whenever possible, goose flighting took pride of place, with duck a close second, the sporting little "goldies" were not far behind in the popularity stakes; indeed Pat, whose ability to bring these fast fliers to bag left little to be desired, would just as soon have gone after them as anything else. Because of the nature of the country over which we shot the golden plover (an extensive area of almost dead flat fields and merseland) they were, despite their comparative abundance, often extremely difficult to get on terms with, and our tactics had to be varied according to circumstances. A light frost sometimes produced good sport along the tide edge, but a really hard frost could, and often would, clear almost all the plover out of the district in a single night.

In calm, open weather the usual procedure was to try to discover the fields in which the plover were feeding, and then organise a series of impromptu drives. These usually resulted in short, sharp engagements, with the odds very much in favour of the goldies. Sometimes we discovered well-established flight lines from the roosting to the feeding grounds, and by lying in ambush on one of these, we contrived, on occasions, to get sport of a superlative nature. Once again the weather was the vital factor; on a calm morning or with a light wind, the birds would in all probability be much too high to shoot, and although a few could usually be "whistled" within range, sport would generally be very quiet. But sooner or later would come a morning when the birds had to face a stiff head wind, and then the fun would be fast and furious.

At First Light

Just such a morning occurred in the winter of 1955/6. The party consisted of Pat, Julian with his wife Diana, old Bob the professional wildfowler and myself. The original plan had been for a duck flight, but this was cancelled at Bob's suggestion when he predicted with complete accuracy that, with the wind blowing at almost gale force from the north-west, the golden plover would concentrate in the north end of a merse, which was sheltered by a line of trees and a high thorn hedge growing on top of the sea bank. As soon, therefore, as there was sufficient light to see clearly, we made our way out on to the merse and lined up about 100 yards apart in a series of little creeks. Before very long the first of the plover began to flight, most of them flying directly up wind and many just a few yards above the grass. To begin with they arrived singly or in little trips of up to half-a-dozen or so, not easily seen and astonishingly difficult to hit.

The number of kills to cartridges would hardly bear thinking about

Soon the guns were banging away merrily and the battle had commenced. Out on my right, Julian, not being in his best form, fired a considerable number of shots before he connected with anything at all, and then it was a bird flying some way behind the one he aimed at. Having thus discovered that the plover were flying a great deal faster than they appeared to be doing, his shooting improved considerably. Even old Bob, usually a very deadly shot, contrived to miss a surprising number of birds, and at one stage the number of kills to cartridges fired would hardly bear thinking about!

Spectacular Shots

Fortunately Pat was in good form throughout the flight, and pulled off a number of spectacular shots, while I, although far from brilliant, managed to maintain a reasonable average, mainly by avoiding shooting at the more difficult birds, since I had not brought along a very large supply of cartridges.

Mid-morning brought a lull in the battle during which it was discovered that all of us were very low in ammunition and Julian, who had fired almost all his cartridges, volunteered to walk to the nearby town to purchase a fresh supply for all hands. During his absence Diana, who wasn't shooting, joined me in my creek, and shortly afterwards a little trip of four plover flashed past on our right, flying only a few yards above the grass. My shot at the leader brought no less than three of the four bouncing on the grass, and I was so surprised that I failed to get my second barrel off at the survivor. Soon after this a counter flight developed, most of the plover coming either down or across wind in large scattered parties, flying high and fast, and making exciting and difficult shooting.

Ammunition Replenished

By now Bob was out of ammunition, but Pat pulled off some wonderful shots at these high birds, and I added a few to my own account. Eventually Julian arrived back with a large supply of cartridges and a new pair of trousers he had bought at the same time. He also brought the news that the people in the town were wondering if there was a battle going on down on the merse, owing to the almost incessant firing!

For another hour or two the flight continued, with scattered trips of goldies arriving at intervals and circling the area at a good height. Many of these late arrivals, since they were obviously looking for others of their kind with which to join forces, responded well to our very amateur efforts at decoy whistling, and a number paid the penalty. Slowly but surely our bag mounted and when at last we decided to call it a day we found, after a careful pick-up, that we had bagged a total of 59 plover.

As we walked towards the merse edge a single goldie flew piping round. "Whistle him in Robert," quoth Pat, "and I'll try to bring our total up to a nice round 60." Old Bob duly obliged, and as the plover circled high overhead, Pat brought him down with a splendid shot.

FERRYMAN'S ARCTIC ADVENTURE

A hazardous sortie after Wigeon

FOLLOWING the blizzard of two days previously, the land lay under a deep covering of snow. Great floes of frozen snow and ice swept up and down the river as the tides ebbed and flowed. On our own side of the estuary the merseland lay under a dirty white mantle of frozen snow and slush, for, although the tide had been above the level of the grass, the snow was so deep that it only floated on the surface of the water, and when the tide ebbed away it froze into an icy mass that covered almost every inch of grass. On the other side, however, the wind and tide had swept certain areas clear of snow, and through the glasses I could see large numbers of wigeon feeding in these patches. It was a fowler's dream come true!

All outdoor work having ceased, I was free to go after the wildfowl if only I could get there ; but this was easier said than done. In those days my sole means of transport was a pushbike, my friend Bob, the owner of " James " the motorbike, having died in tragic circumstances some time previously. In any case, the roads were completely blocked by deep drifts, so if I was to reach this bonanza it would have to be by water.

Inevitably I consulted my friend Adam. " Well," quoth he, after studying the ice-packed river through his glasses, " you can borrow the black punt, but you'll hae tae be very careful wi' a' that ice aboot. Wait until very near low water when the run'll be aff the tide, it should be safe enough tae cross then, and mind," he added, " be back on this side before flood tide, or the ice'll sweep you up the river and ye'll be in hubble street for sure."

Promising to do exactly as he told me, I made immediate preparations for departure. The black punt, locally known as. " The Coffin," was lying in a handy place, so as soon as I had all my gear assembled, I dug her out of the snow, launched her and worked her down through the ice and slush to the mouth of the mooring creek. As the tide fell, ice jams began to form in the river, and just before low water a jam formed at a jetty about a couple of hundred yards upstream, leaving a long stretch of almost ice-free water below it. Taking advantage of this I rowed across and anchored the punt behind the jetty immediately below the ice jam. In this position I was close to the mouth of the Judge's Burn, along the edge of which I had previously noted a large number of wigeon feeding on an area of exposed grass. It had been my intention to stalk some of these birds, and I would probably have succeeded, but, as I crept round the corner of the burn mouth, a couple of redshank sprang up, screaming their heads off.

For a second or two nothing happened and then, with a roar of wings, a mass of wigeon rose off the grass above and beyond me and swinging round behind, pitched in the ice-free part of the river. As soon as they were all safely down I hurried towards the area in which they had been feeding, it was easily enough found for it was a solid mass of droppings. Panting with exertion and excitement, I looked around for somewhere to hide and quickly settled on a niche among some tumbled slabs of frozen snow, right on the edge of the burn and within range of one of the likeliest looking grassy areas. I knew I wouldn't have long to wait before some of the wigeon returned to their feeding place, and, sure enough, in about ten minutes or so, a large company came whipping up over the sea-wall and headed straight for my position.

I fired as they circled to land, using a conspicuous cock as an aiming mark for my first shot. Down he went, and four others along with him, and as the survivors flared I knocked down another couple with my second shot. Hastily reloading, I looked towards the river and saw that the shots had put the entire mass of wigeon on the wing. One party

"Be back on this side before flood tide, or the ice'll sweep you up the river . . . ."

swung in towards the burn mouth, and as they passed behind me I shot a couple which fell on the opposite side of the burn. Again I reloaded without moving from my stance, and as another party that had circled inland came out over my head, I fired again, missing with my first shot, and killing another duck with my second. This bird also fell on the far side of the burn, and it now occurred to me that these birds were going to be very difficult to recover. Under normal conditions I would simply have rowed the punt into the burn mouth, and waded ashore ; but conditions were not normal, and this procedure was virtually impossible owing to the ice jam below which the punt was moored. The burn could not be forded, so I would have to use the cattle bridge which was at least half a mile away. This would mean a walk of over two miles before I could reach the duck and return to

66

the punt. I had calculated, when I arrived, that I could risk waiting 12 hours, but no longer. It was absolutely vital that I should be back across the river before the flood tide set in. I looked at my watch. I had about an hour left ; if I was going after the wigeon I would have to go soon.

As these thoughts passed through my mind, I had been engaged in picking up the seven wigeon which had fallen on my own side of the burn. Two of these had only been winged and I spent some minutes looking for them, but eventually found them hiding in a tiny creek that ran through the snow-free area. Returning to my original position I decided to wait for about ten minutes and then set out to recover the duck on the far side of the burn. Although the bulk of the wigeon had cleared off, there were still several small parties flying around, and presently one of these pitched just out of range of my position and commenced feeding. It was impossible for me to get any closer to these birds, and as the minutes ticked away I began to get worried . . . . I simply couldn't afford to wait any longer ; if I was going after my remaining birds I would have to go now ! I stole one last look at the wigeon, they were tantalizingly close, but not quite close enough. However, they were inshore of me and if disturbed would most probably make straight for the river, thus offering me a passing shot. I decided to disturb them !

Pointing the gun downward and away from the duck I fired into the mud and slush and turned just as the wigeon whipped out past me. At my shot two dropped dead in front of me, and another, hard hit, turned out across the burn and planed down on to the far bank. Carefully noting the position of this bird, I hastily gathered the remaining two and stuffed them into the bag with the rest, then leaving everything behind except my gun and a few spare cartridges, I set out for the cattle bridge. Before I had gone very far I realised just what I had let myself in for. The thigh-deep snow had in most places been quite unaffected by the tide, and ploughing through this was laborious in the extreme. By the time I reached the cattle bridge I was already pretty fagged, but, having always made a point of retrieving shot birds whenever possible, I somewhat uneasily, and against my better judgment, decided to carry on.

On the far side of the burn the going was somewhat better though still very difficult, but there was no time to rest so I pressed on at my best speed. As I neared the spot where the duck lay I noticed several greater black-back gulls pulling at something, and fearing for my wigeon I fired a shot to scare them away. My fears were well founded—three of the duck were completely ruined, one being little more than a skeleton, and two others having most of their breasts eaten off. The remaining duck, the last one I had shot, was still alive and unmarked, having been partly concealed and apparently overlooked by the gulls. After all my toil, this was a bitter disappointment but time marched relentlessly on, so after a brief rest I hurried, back the way I had come. Having " broken trail " as it were, on the outward journey, the return was somewhat easier, but I was rapidly running out of time and as I ploughed along in a lather of sweat I cast many an anxious glance at my watch.

On reaching my cache, I was compelled to take another breather before gathering up my gear and hurrying off to the river's edge. As I topped the sea-wall an alarming sight greeted me. I was too late, the ice-covered tide was already sweeping up the river in an irresistible flood ! Hastily dumping my gear in the punt I returned to the top of the sea-wall and looked down the estuary : there was little comfort there, for as far as the eye could see the surface of the water was almost completely covered with ice. Anxiously I watched the flood sweep past,

I felt myself growing dizzy as the floes swept relentlessly past

the floes hissing and crackling as they came in contact with each other. Now and then open spaces formed as the powerful eddies swirled the ice floes this way and that, and finally I decided that the next time a reasonable lead opened up I would push off and try to force a way through. Time and again likely looking leads closed before they came opposite the punt. I felt myself growing dizzy as I watched the ice sweep relentlessly past ; then, at last, a clear space opened up at just the right moment and I was off !

Rowing with all my strength, I shot the punt obliquely across the open lead and managed to cover about half the width of the main river channel before the ice packed tight around the punt, making it impossible to use the oars. It was a weird experience sitting there locked in the mass of ice ; if one looked only at the ice the punt appeared to be stationary, and only by looking at the banks could one appreciate the speed and power of the current that was sweeping the entire mass along. Ahead of me another jetty thrust out into the river, and I noticed that the eddies and turbulence caused by it were breaking up the ice masses just as the one behind which I had been anchored had done. Shipping one oar, I knelt facing forward and with the other oar held like a paddle, prepared to take advantage of every lead or open space the eddies might produce. Soon I was in the area of turbulence, and as the ice mass loosened up I pushed, thrust, and paddled for all I was worth, gradually edging nearer and nearer the safety of the water's edge. Fearing that I would again be swept out of the area of loose ice, I managed to turn the punt's bow until it was facing the tide, and although I couldn't possibly hold my position against the current, by working like a Trojan, I managed to edge nearer and nearer to the shore. By now I was rapidly nearing complete exhaustion, so much so that when my oar finally touched bottom I was able only to jump overboard and stand there hanging on to the punt and gasping for breath; as the ice bumped past around my legs.

Finally I towed the punt ashore and, after a long rest, " walked " it down the edge of the tide to the mooring creek which was also full of ice, and eventually up the creek to the anchorage, by which time I felt fine and ready for the next adventure on the morrow.

CHANGE OF LUCK

LADY Luck, as everyone knows, is a fickle jade, and no matter with what ardour one may woo her, she is capable on occasions, of dealing out a distressing number of rebuffs. I know not in what way we had offended her, but for all too long a period recently, she defied and frustrated all our attempts to come to terms with the geese, and only relented somewhat grudgingly in the end.

No matter where we went, the geese either went elsewhere or tantalised us by passing, or even pitching, just out of range. If it was a matter of choosing

Skein after skein swept up the estuary

one of two positions, we were sure to choose the wrong one. If we changed our position, the geese flew slap over the one we had just vacated. If we decided to stay put, they passed within easy shot of the one we had considered an alternative. Time and again we had them right overhead, just a little too high, or had them turned by another gun when coming straight at us at shootable height. It was all very frustrating, but, since we wooed her persistently, Lady Luck in the end relented, but grudgingly, as I have said before.

The first sign occurred one morning when I accidentally met my old friend Bob, the one time professional wildfowler, while waiting for the geese to flight. The morning, as so many have been this season, was calm and still and unseasonably mild, so to increase my slender chances I had set up a dozen wooden decoys in the hope of tempting an unwary goose within range. In the early morning dusk I spotted the stocky figure of my friend coming along the sea bank, and in answer to my hail, he joined me in my hideout. At my invitation he willingly agreed to give me the pleasure of his company, and to share the benefit of the decoys.

Denture Drill

In due course, several skeins of grey-lags appeared heading inland at such a height as to merit hardly a second glance. Later some pinkfeet appeared, and although Bob called hopefully at them and received a reply, they decided to carry on to wherever they were going. A few minutes later another lot of pink-feet appeared in a long, straggly line. Again Bob called lustily at them (taking out his top dentures to do so, as he reckons he can get a better sound this way !), and again they chose to ignore both he and the decoys—all, that is, except one.

Why this goose chose to desert the skein and turn back to the call of a human voice, and a stand of three-ply silhouettes, is impossible to say. Perhaps it was just Lady Luck beginning to relent; in any case, turn back it did, and old Bob nearly choked in his efforts to call it down to the decoys. More like a pigeon than a goose, the pinkfoot zoomed down in a long curve, set its wings, put down its paddles, and suddenly there it was within 25 yards of us and obviously about to pitch among the decoys. " He's all yours, Robert," I whispered, and the next second his old and well-used gun had done its duty. I was well enough rewarded by his words of praise for the fine retrieve carried out by my young bitch, Candy: Old Bob is somewhat spare with his praise for either man or dog !

A few mornings later her Ladyship smiled a brief and belated smile upon me personally. Once again alone I had gone to a spot well up the estuary in the hope that by the time they had flown this far, some of the geese would be looking for a place to land. The weather continued mild and somewhat misty, with daylight reluctant to come. The geese flighted early—a lot of geese—and skein after skein swept up the estuary, lines of vague smudges against the dark sky. Each time I heard their voices approaching, my heartbeats quickened, and I thought " this is it, surely this lot will be within shot." But no ! The pattern remained as before, those which passed overhead were all too high and any that were low enough were too far out over the river. Gradually the darkness yielded to the rising sun, and as the morning lengthened

I once again resigned myself to carrying home my gun, its mirrors undimmed. I looked at my watch—I would give it another quarter of an hour, and then pack up: and during this period they came, right down the river from behind me, eight greylags, flying straight at me, and less than 40 yards high !

Hastily covering Candy with her sack lest her light colour catch the keen eyes of the geese, I crouched in my creek and waited for them. On they came as though they intended to fly right over my head, then, to my dismay, they began to swing out towards the river. Desperately I called to them, and once again they changed course, but now they were going to pass on my right, a long shot but a reasonable one. The charge from the 3in. BB. caught the nearest goose fair and square, and down he went. As the survivors climbed I fired at the next bird, but probably shot right underneath it, as the shot had no visible effect. Candy brought the dead goose to hand and as I took it from her I felt a lifting of the spirit, and the previously dreary morning suddenly took on a new look.

Four days later, my confidence restored, I returned to the same place, having the previous evening predicted to my highly sceptical wife that, given a strong head wind, I would this time bring her back four, perhaps even six geese ! I need hardly add that this was to boost my own morale as much as anything else. The morning to my great disappointment was completely windless, but having once again taken the decoys, I felt that this did not necessarily mean that it was hopeless. Having assembled and set up the decoys, I took cover in the same creek as before and waited—and waited. An hour went past during which time I neither heard nor saw a single goose. Soon it was broad daylight, and I was just thinking of packing up when I heard the distant sound of geese. Picking up the binoculars I looked to seaward . . . the entire sky seemed to be laced with geese as skein after skein swept up the estuary.

Fantastic Din

Quite evidently all the geese had come off the sands in one great " lift." The first to arrive was a massive skein of pinkfeet, flying in a great arc-shaped mass. The centre of the arc came straight over my head at a height of about 80 yards, gabbling and calling in their high-pitched voices, and creating a din that was quite fantastic. Soon the sky overhead was filled with geese . . . geese arriving, geese circling, and all the time the incessant din of a thousand voices. Some of the circling geese were now almost in range, and as I watched through my face mask I was torn between the urge to take whatever chance came my way, or to continue to watch this fantastic spectacle. Wedged between my knees I could feel Candy tremble violently under her sack, doubtless puzzled by the din and my inaction.

For a time it seemed certain that at least some of the geese would pitch in the vicinity of the decoys. But they must have spotted the deception, for suddenly the lower echelons climbed back to their original height, and the whole mass swept up the estuary, but without showing any signs of panic. I was just about to straighten my aching back when I spotted four geese returning and losing height rapidly. Soon they were circling the decoys, and as they swung round behind me I stood up and fired at the nearest bird. A hit. . . . ! The goose staggered, but continued to fly . . . a second shot and it crumpled up and crashed to the ground. Candy brought it in, a young and very small pinkfoot.

Some time later another skein of about 20 pinks came back down the estuary, and after circling the decoys once or twice, set their wings and straight in towards me. I was all set to give them a warm reception when they braked and pitched, just a little too far away for a shot. My heart sank, there was no way in which I could get any closer unless perhaps Taking the BB. cartridges from the magnum, I replaced them with a couple of treble A's, then, leaving Candy at the drop, I climbed carefully on to a small ledge in the creek, took a deep breath, sprang over the edge and dashed towards the geese at top speed !

The geese took off with understandable alacrity, so sliding to a halt I fired when they were about 20 feet above the ground, and to my joy one bird fell stone dead, shot clean through the head and neck. At my shout Candy raced out and brought the goose, a really splendid pinkfoot, young and broad of breast . . . a worthy gift from Lady Luck.

CANDY'S FIRST

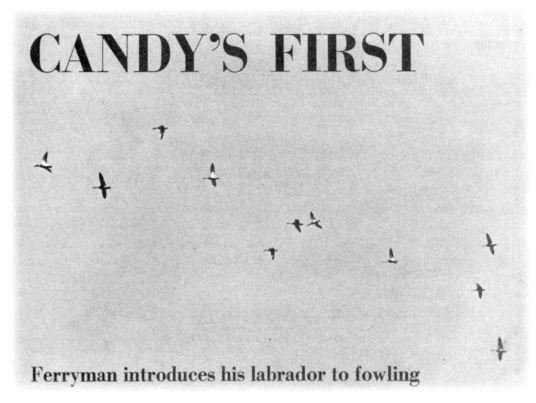

Ferryman introduces his labrador to fowling

. . . . just too high to shoot at.

D. N. Dalton

BOTH my son Howard and I had looked forward to this particular outing with more than ordinary anticipation, for this was to be Candy's very first wildfowling expedition. Candy is our new Labrador puppy. The colour of clotted cream, with golden ears and hackles; she is a very lovely creature indeed, and this, allied to the fact that she has a most endearing disposition, has mitigated somewhat against the rigorous training schedule we had planned for her. Indeed, we have been compelled to fight a tactful, yet almost continuous rearguard action against the subversive activities of the female members of the family, not always, I admit, with complete success! Nevertheless, her training has so far gone surprisingly well, so much so, that after one or two preliminary outings on which she acquitted herself creditably, we decided to take her out on a full scale morning flight the next time Howard was at home for the weekend.

So it came about that one morning in early November with an excited puppy sitting in the back of the car, we set out for one of our favourite places, picking up Howard's friend Hugh at his home *en route*. It was a pleasant enough morning, but not one to inspire a great deal of hope, being almost windless with a clear sky and a light frost; but we hoped at the very least for a shot or two in the dawn light. Our chosen venue was a wide stretch of sand and shingle across which meandered a burn, the clear waters of which, although wide, were usually only a few inches deep. This was often a favourite flight line for mallard heading seaward from their inland feeding grounds, while the burn itself was sometimes visited by other duck including wigeon, pintail and teal. The outstanding disadvantage of the place was the almost total lack of natural cover, for apart from one or two pebble ridges of no great height, and a small but somewhat higher mussel scaur, the place was flat and featureless.

Over the years we had tried all sorts of tricks to produce the necessary cover, even constructing portable hides made from various materials such as netting, hessian etc., but with little success. Although we kept these erections as low as possible they were visible for miles, and few duck ventured within range. Digging in on these stony flats likewise proved to be of little avail. It was extremely difficult to do so, and, in any case, the holes quickly filled with water, making frequent bailing necessary. However, the mussel scaur proved to be a much better proposition, and on this we found we could construct serviceable, though very uncomfortable hides, by digging shallow pits, banking up the excavated material and topping this with any seaweed we could find lying around. By crouching, and I really mean crouching, in these, we have on occasions enjoyed excellent sport, the duck taking little or no notice of them. Shooting from these hides is very difficult, as one has to remain motionless until the last possible moment, and then, as often as not, shoot while kneeling on one or both knees.

Having left home in good time it was still quite dark when we arrived at our destination, and after climbing into our fowling gear, we set out to walk the mile or so across the flats to our fighting spot. About halfway across ran another watercourse, and here I decided to remain with the dog as long as it was dark enough to offer some concealment. In the meantime, the boys would carry on to the mussel scaur where I would join them later. Kneeling in a fold in the pebble ridge, my gamebag propped up in front of me to help break up my silhouette, I watched and waited, but the only sign or sound of duck was the distant quacking of some mallard and the occasional whicker of wings as duck passed overhead, too high to be seen.

70

Gradually the dark sky turned to grey and fighting gulls appeared as black silhouettes as they ghosted past, but still not a duck had I seen; then I noticed Candy stiffen and gaze intently up the watercourse. Slipping the binoculars from their case I focused them in that direction; sure enough a single duck of some kind was swimming downstream towards me. Waiting until I could see it vaguely with the naked eye I stood up, and as the duck leapt from the water I fired, missing it with my first barrel, but knocking it down, a runner, with my second. Candy was on to it in a flash, and although the duck attempted to dive, the shallow water made this difficult and she was back with it in a couple of minutes, a splendid retrieve of her first duck under " active service " conditions.

I was somewhat disappointed to find I had shot a merganser, a bird I would not normally have attempted to shoot, but at any rate my shots appeared to have stirred something up, for immediately afterwards I heard two shots from the boys' direction, soon followed by four more. Quite soon it was clear enough to see through the binoculars that the boys were occupying the same hide and I was rather puzzled by this. Later I discovered that a recent storm had washed away most of the mussel scaur, leaving a small island, sufficient only for one hide. As I watched, two more shots rang out, and I saw one of the boys leave the hide and pick up something . . . evidently they were having some success. During the next 20 minutes or so, although I heard a shot or two from the boys, nothing else came my way, and by the end of this time the light had improved to such an extent that I was compelled to move. When I rejoined the boys I was delighted to find that they had already bagged four pintail and three wigeon. I was equally pleased to find that on discovering there was room for only one hide, they had made it big enough for all three of us!

Shortly after I joined them a single pintail flew high and fast down the burn towards us, and at the boys' insistence I took it as it passed over the hide. It staggered at the shot but turned at right angles and carried on for about 300 yards before plummeting stone-dead to the sands. Taking Candy across the burn, Howard sent her out and after a bit of dashing about, she found and retrieved the pintail, a fine drake not yet in full plumage. Our next real excitement was a team of four mallard flying downstream from the land. In the windless conditions prevailing, almost everything except the mergansers was flying high, and these were no exception. Nevertheless, there was no excuse for the completely fruitless volley that saluted them as they passed overhead, and we were somewhat shamefaced about it. Candy was highly indignant and obviously puzzled when she was not allowed to go out and retrieve something after all that noise!

To restore our morale we decided to have our tea and sandwiches, so flasks and sandwich-boxes were dug out of gamebags, tea poured out and the interior of the hide liberally strewn with all this impedimenta when another team of four mallard was seen approaching. Dropping everything we seized our guns and prepared for action, the two boys as usual to fire to their front or appropriate side, as the case may be, and I to fire to the rear. Again the duck were high, but not too high, but despite the boys' shots all four were still going strong when they came into my line of vision as I faced the rear. I fired at the last bird in the line, a large drake, killing him with the only shot I got off. He fell with a tremendous thud on the hard sand, and when Candy brought him in, in great style, we found the skin completely split off one side of the breast. The tide was now flowing strongly and several parties of duck, both wigeon, mallard and pintail, passed up or down the burn. All of these were just too high to shoot at : Oh for a good stiff breeze!

In the distance two girls on ponies came galloping across the sands and we had just decided to call it a day when three mallard, probably disturbed by the girls, came flying down the burn towards us. As they passed on his left, Howard knocked down a couple, and I downed the survivor as it fled to the rear. Two of the duck fell in the burn and the other on the far bank, and Candy, noticing that this bird was still alive, dropped the dead bird she had already picked up, and splashing across the burn dashed after the cripple. To our delight she retrieved this to hand, and in a few minutes had completed the pick-up, erring only in dropping one bird in order to shake herself as she emerged from the burn, before picking it up again and bringing it to hand. Altogether a most satisfactory ending to an exciting and enjoyable morning, and full marks to a promising young dog.

THE WHITE DUCK

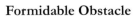

OUR first encounter with the white duck resulted in a disappointment of such magnitude that my friend and companion Bob, who was more than a little superstitious, declared that this unfortunate bird was in some way responsible, and that the sooner we got rid of it the better! It is doubtful if he really believed this, but nevertheless from that day onward he kept a sharp lookout for the white duck and put himself to a great deal of trouble in trying to locate it.

Our daylight activities at that time being largely confined to Saturday afternoon outings, we had taken the punt out on the flood tide in the hope of falling in with some duck in the upper tidal reaches of the estuary. A strong and bitterly cold east wind was blowing, whipping the brown water of the estuary into a choppy sea which broke in sheets of spray along the lee shore. Only the fact that we were on the windward side made it possible to operate at all, and even then conditions were, to say the least, very difficult.

Formidable Obstacle

For the first mile or so nothing of special interest was seen, and then, upon rounding a bend, we spotted a dark mass of birds sitting on the steeply sloping mud of the river bank about half a mile ahead. They had the appearance of duck, and a quick look through the glasses confirmed this. We made immediate preparations to attack! While Bob loaded the puntgun (a small breech-loader, borrowed from our friend Adam, and firing 8 oz of BB shot)

I laid out a couple of setting poles of different lengths and a pair of hand paddles. The latter would be necessary to negotiate a formidable obstacle which lay a short distance ahead—a stone jetty, round which the tide ran strongly and in the vicinity of which the water was very rough. As soon as everything was ready, Bob lay down behind the gun, and I, who had undertaken to " set " the punt, lay down in the stern, picked up a setting pole, and we were off! The approach was difficult in the extreme, the strong off-shore wind constantly

Bob was convinced it was a jinx, recalls Ferryman

threatening to blow the punt out into the deep water where we would immediately have lost control. Indeed, this almost happened as we rounded the jetty, and only a fortuitous eddy swept us close enough to the shore to enable me to regain control.

Difficult Approach

The duck were now only about a quarter of a mile ahead of us, so Bob got out the glasses to have another look. " What are they, Bob? " I asked, " are they wigeon? " After a pause Bob replied, " I can't see very well with the punt jumping up and down like this, but I'm almost certain they're mallard! There appears to he about 50 or 60 of them! " This was surprising news, for although there were usually some mallard in this part of the river, they rarely congregated in groups as large as this one. " They all appear to be sound asleep," added Bob in rising excitement, " for goodness sake don't let the punt blow offshore, we'll never get another chance like this! " Promising to do my best I struggled with might and main to keep the punt as close as possible to the edge. This was vitally necessary, for had we blown off, even a few yards, it would have been impossible to reach the bottom with the setting-pole; this would have resulted in the punt blowing out into mid-river in a few seconds.

Slowly we crept closer and closer as I thrust and toiled with the setting pole; the water was now alarmingly rough, and the punt wallowed through the waves which swept her entire length, from time to time drenching us with showers of icy water which splashed over the coaming. Despite the fact that Bob had the gun elevator pulled back as far as possible, and the gun muzzle literally pointing to the sky, there was the constant danger that, as the punt's bow fell into a trough, a wave would fill the muzzle with water, but fortunately this did not happen.

" Almost in range now," breathed Bob over his shoulder, and I could feel his right leg tremble with excitement. " Try to keep her head a wee bit inshore if you possibly can so that I can get the gun to bear." " Sorry, old boy, can't be done," I gasped. " I'll have to hold her on this course until the last possible moment, and then swing her round."
" O.K.," replied Bob, " you're doing fine."

Yard by yard we crept nearer . . . . now the duck were in plain view even from my prone position in the stern of the punt. So steep was the slope of the mud that had the duck been awake they would have been able to see right down into the cockpit. Well, in a few more seconds it wouldn't matter whether they awoke or not.

" Range," hissed Bob. " Right," I replied, pushing the stern of the punt outward so that her bow swung in towards the duck. As I did so I glanced upwards . . . . every bird was awake, and standing with neck at full stretch. " Too late," I thought in triumph, " we have you ! "

The next instant they were in the air, a great brown ball of birds, impossible to miss. I saw the muzzle of the gun swing out to intercept them and set myself for the crash of the shot. At that precise moment the punt's bow dropped with astonishing suddenness into a trough and a great brown wave reared up in front of us, at the same instant as the gun went off and I distinctly saw the smother of spray as the shot tore through it. In stunned disbelief we watched the mallard swing out over the river ; conspicuous among them was something we had not noticed before . . . . a snow-white duck, its plumage glinting like silver in the wintry sunshine. We watched in stricken silence until they disappeared from sight. Not a single duck was down, the wave had apparently swallowed the entire charge !

Jinx Laid Low

Several weeks later Bob came to me in a state of suppressed excitement. " I know where the white mallard is," said he. " How about going after it this afternoon if you have nothing else on ? " Knowing that nothing would put him off, I agreed to accompany him, and early that afternoon we cautiously approached a tributary burn, not very far from the scene of our abortive puntgun shot. With guns at the ready we tiptoed to the edge of the bank and peeped over— nothing. The stretch of water visible to us contained not so much as a redshank !

"Perhaps it's further up," said Bob doggedly. "Anyhow, I'm sure it's about here somewhere. The shepherd told me he had put it out of this part of the burn several times recently, and he promised not to come near the place this morning." " Righto, Bob," said I, " you go on up the burn and I'll wait here at the mouth, and if it is up there, and you miss it, I'll be in a good position here to intercept it." " I won't miss it," said Bob grimly, and off he went. Taking cover in some tall reeds I watched him plod up the burnside and cautiously approach the next bend. Chuckling to myself at his keenness, I thought, " Oh well, I suppose there is a possibility of the white duck being there, but it's a pretty dim one." Then I saw Bob stiffen, and a moment later seven mallard appeared above the top of the reeds, and among them, almost unbeliev-ably, the white duck !

The seven birds climbed rapidly away, and then began to turn towards the river. I heard a single shot ring out and at the same instant the white duck folded up and plummetted into the reed bed. Halfway up the burnside I met Bob returning with his prize. " I got him," he remarked needlessly, handing me the white duck. " That's the last time he'll jinx us or anybody else ! "

Later we examined the bird carefully ; apart from some staining on the breast and underparts, probably due to contact with mud or peat-stained water, the plumage was pure white, without a trace of pigment. Although in flight it had appeared larger than its normal coloured companions, we were surprised to find that it was a comparatively small bird, and this despite the fact that a somewhat undeveloped curl in the tail indicated that it was a drake. This was later confirmed by the museum to which we presented the bird.

The Final Fling

Ferryman recalls a red-letter day at the end of last season

WITH all the excitement and anticipation of a new season before us we can forget, or at any rate forgive, the disasters and disappointments that beset many of us during the previous season, and look back for inspiration on any good days that may have come our way. I, myself, was fortunate in having several such days, not least the very last one of the season. Having been " under the weather " for some time previously I very nearly didn't go out at all, and only because it was the last day did I sally forth for a final fling.

From a fowlers point of view the weather could hardly have been better. A strong and bitter wind lashed the sea, almost guaranteeing that the duck would be kept on the move. Being unable to raise a companion owing to it being mid-week, dawn found me, accompanied by my Labrador Candy, ensconced in a hide well sheltered from the wind by a large bed of reeds. On my right as I faced seaward, flowed the waters of a little tidal stream on which floated my four rubber decoys, and on a ledge to my left Candy lay snuggled down on a thick bed of dried grass, placed there for her comfort. I would have preferred to have been much further seaward but this would have meant exposing myself to the bitter wind which, in view of a recent illness, I thought unwise.

The first arrivals were three mallard which appeared out of the gloom at no great height, flying straight into the teeth of the wind. My two shots had no visible effect, much to the disgust of Candy, who had instantly sprung to attention. Soon after a mallard drake flew " yeeping " past, and again I missed with both barrels. Cursing under my breath I reloaded just in time to get off two more abortive shots at a pair of duck which I recognised as pintail as they flared to the shots. All this was somewhat demoralising and when three more mallard appeared, I was so surprised when one fell dead to my first shot that the survivors flew off unsaluted !

Shortly after this minor success the geese started to flight, but although I had several lots right over my head, they were all just a little too high for a shot. These birds were coming with the wind in their tails and were travelling at an astonishing speed. As each skein passed over I took a practice swing at them and concluded that even had they been low enough they would have been extremely difficult to hit. From the point of view of spectacle this was one of the most interesting flights I have ever witnessed. The geese, all of them greylags, were coming in parties of up to 50 or 60 on a comparatively narrow front, so that most passed quite close to my position, hurtling along like giant leaves before the gale.

I was so engrossed in watching the geese that a small party of wigeon flying seaward against the wind were actually past me before I saw them. A couple of hasty snap-shots and two drakes splashed into the burn. As Candy raced out to retrieve I quickly reloaded and glanced over my shoulder—another party of wigeon was almost on top of me. Two more shots and two more wigeon splashed into the burn, one landing almost on top of the dog, who very intelligently added it to the one she had already picked up, bringing both birds ashore at once. No sooner were the four wigeon safely in the bag than a pair of mallard appeared, battling against the wind. These birds were somewhat wide of me but, spotting the decoys, they swept in with the obvious intention of pitching beside them. As soon as they were close enough I stood up and fired as they flared against the now clear sky. They dropped, each on the far side of the burn, and Candy quickly added them to the nicely growing bag.

The next arrival was a single teal, and having accounted for him with a good shot I was just about to send the dog out when a scattered party of wigeon appeared in the distance. These birds passed inshore of the hide and this time I succeeded in knocking down three. By now I felt on top of the world—despite a bad start I had bagged 11 duck with my last 10 shots, a standard well above my usual . .. now if only I could bag a goose. . .. I glanced at the two BB cartridges lying on the game bag in front of me.

Although the main flight had ceased some time previously, a few odd geese continued to appear from seaward. These I watched eagerly in the hope that at least some of them would be low enough for a shot. Eventually four greylags appeared, flying straight at me at what I considered just about shootable height. Quickly loading with the BBs, I waited until they were almost straight overhead, stood up and swung on the nearest bird—and what a swing that was ! By the time the gun muzzles had caught up with it, the goose was well past and the one shot I managed to get off appeared to have no effect at all. Seconds later, however, he swerved away from the other three and, turning to face the wind, came back towards me, losing height rapidly. Eventually he landed about 150 yards away in a patch of long, rough grass in which I couldn't spot him even with the aid of binoculars. I was in something of a quandary—there was no way of reaching the spot unseen, and if I approached openly he might well get up and fly away before I was within range ; I decided to send the dog in. Candy knew very well where the goose was and dashed straight to the spot, while I watched anxiously. I needn't have worried ; after a deal of "lifting and laying" until she had it properly balanced, she came trotting back with a huge greylag ; it was stone dead.

Thoroughly delighted I decided that the right moment had arrived to have my tea and sandwiches. I was in the middle of this pleasant occupation when a single pintail drake hove in sight. He passed me within easy range and as I put the gun up I never for a moment doubted that he would collapse at the first shot. Perhaps it was just as well for my now somewhat inflated ego that he carried on untouched by either of my two shots !

Considerably chastened, I finished my tea and shortly afterwards fate relented once again. A party of about a dozen pintail came whizzing in from the sea and, having gone a few hundred yards past my position, decided to turn back. In doing so they presented me with a first-class chance. This time I made no mistake, and soon Candy presented me with a fine pair including an adult drake in magnificent plumage. Had I been positioned half a mile or so further seaward, there is little doubt that I would have added several more of these fine duck to the bag, as I could see considerable numbers, together with some wigeon, flighting into the merse.

The morning was now well advanced and I was just thinking of packing up when another pair of mallard came flying down the burn and headed for the decoys. These birds came in so low that they momentarily disappeared below the bank of the burn, and when they reappeared they were little more than 15 yards from me. Resisting the temptation to fire too soon, I waited until they were about 35 yards away and dropped them one after the other, to complete a bag of 15 duck and one goose, and conclude a magnificent morning's sport.

Memorable Shot

The day when, Ferryman writes, everything went according to plan

THE date in my diary is Monday, January 16, 1956. The entry reads as follows :

"Went out alone at 5.30 a.m. in punt. Shot three greylags with two shots (12-bore) on Grant's Point at daybreak. Later passed up two chances at geese with puntgun in the hope of a big shot at wigeon. Justified. Had a grand shot opposite the Judge's Burn mouth ; bagged 59 wigeon and lost two others which were eaten by gulls ; had some trouble with cripples owing to swift current."

Looking back over the events of which this entry is the bare bones, it was easy to recall each incident of that memorable morning, including the hectic cripple chase hinted at in the last sentence. The prime purpose of the early start was to enable me to push upstream in the dark, and have the punt in such a position that any duck pitching in or alongside the tidal river below me would show up clearly against the dawn light, while the punt, approaching as it would be from the dark area, would be very difficult to see. In addition I would then have the advantage of the current which ran very strongly at this state of the tide.

There was nothing new about this plan which was by far the most successful method of dealing with this particular reach of the river, and had paid off many times previously . . . not, that it was an easy place in which to punt, far from it. Along one side the river bank was buttressed by a number of stone jetties, built to prevent erosion. Apart from the danger they presented, particularly in the dark, their presence made it almost impossible to punt on that side of the river. On the other side, however, the ebbing tide uncovered a series of mudbanks, alongside which it was possible to work the punt, always providing one did not run aground on any of a number of shallow spits or lose touch with the bottom where the current had dug deep channels close to the edge.

On emerging from the mooring creek I found sufficient tide left to enable me to push up the secondary channel, known as the " Gut," to join the main river at a point well above where I hoped the duck would pitch when they came down off the merselands at daybreak. This was a great saving in time and effort as it cut out the long hard push round the main river channel and resulted in my arriving at my destination long before there was any prospect of dawn. Anchoring the punt at a spot where the bottom was firm and hard, I loaded the big muzzle-loading gun, made everything ready for action, and settled down to wait. Quite soon I became aware that this was one of those odd mornings when small parties of geese were on the wing long before there was the faintest trace of dawn. The first party caught me completely by surprise, the only sound I heard from them being the swish of their wings as they passed so close that they were momentarily visible as darker smudges against the dark sky. Indeed I was still speculating if, in fact, they were geese, when a single quiet call confirmed it. During the next hour or so several other small parties were moving about, but although I now sat with a loaded 12-bore across my knees, I was unable to catch even a single glimpse of them though some must have passed within easy range.

At last a slight paling of the eastern sky indicated that dawn wasn't very far away, and just then a single call announced the arrival of still another lot of geese. Cocking both barrels of the gun, I watched intently in the direction of the sound. Seconds later a line of smudges appeared to my left front at close range, and as they drew level I fired right down their line. The flash of the shot momentarily blinded me and my second shot was taken more or less at random. I had no idea whether or not I had connected, so as the geese went gabbling off into the gloom I seized the torch, waded ashore and shone the light in the direction in which I had fired. Two geese lay dead, almost side by side. and as I flashed the light around I spotted a third walking away from the scene of the fray, trailing a broken wing. All three were quickly collected and stowed away in the punt, and I returned to my vigil. I felt on top of the world. What a start to my morning's sport—my heart sang, and there wasn't a happier man in Britain ! But now I had an important decision to make ; if I went on firing with my 12-bore I would almost certainly spoil my chances of getting a shot with the puntgun. Very soon now the wigeon would be leaving their nocturnal feeding grounds and if any had intended coming to this part of the estuary the sound of none too distant gunfire might change their minds. I decided to shoot at nothing else, no matter how tempting the chance, so, unloading the 12-bore, I stowed it under the gun deck.

Shortly afterwards I heard more geese approaching, and as the reflection of the paling sky was now turning the water a cold steel grey, I lay down in the bottom of the punt lest the oncoming geese spot my silhouette. This party was a little more vocal than their predecessors, and I was able to keep track of them by sound. They were obviously flying very low and coming straight at me. Suddenly there was a splashing sound a short distance down river, and when I looked through the binoculars I could see that the geese, eight of them, had pitched in the water and were swimming ashore not more than 150 yards from the muzzle of the gun ! Here was a pretty pickle—to do or not to do, that was the question ! Soon the geese were standing in the shallows washing and preening, and I had no doubt that I could shoot most, if not all of them, as they were standing in an almost dead straight line. I was sorely tempted to have a go, and very nearly did so but decided in the end to await developments.

A few minutes later another little party arrived and pitched even closer than the first lot, and again I was torn by the urge to accept this gift from the gods. It isn't easy to lie behind a loaded puntgun and watch greylags that could be reached in a minute or two with almost complete certainty. Again I decided to do nothing for the time being. Shortly afterwards I heard wigeon whistling in the distance and saw a black mass of birds drop into the river at the point where I had all along hoped and expected them to pitch.

A mass of wigeon

This was it ! If they came ashore where I hoped they would, they could hardly be in a better place. The curve of the mud-bank would conceal the punt until almost the last minute, and once round the bend I would be up to the duck in no time.

It was now necessary to move the geese with the least possible disturbance, so, rising to my knees, I showed myself briefly, and then lay down again. The geese had spotted me at once and after standing on the alert for a few moments took off and flew down the river, passing right over the position occupied by the wigeon, but without causing any apparent disturbance. In a few seconds I was under way, and, on rounding the bend, found to my joy that the wigeon were all ashore and sitting, as I had hoped, on the sloping mud about 200 yards ahead of me. Although the light was still far from good the black mass of duck was clearly visible against the dawn light, and as I crept closer and closer the old excitement arose in me and I could feel my heartbeats thudding against the floorboards of the punt.

Nearer and nearer I crept ; I had now cocked the action of the gun and with my left hand pressing down on the stock had taken the weight of the gun off the rest. Along the gunbarrel I could just make out the foresight, a vital factor in puntgunning. Aligning this just over the centre of the company I held my course for another 40 yards, let go the setting pole, seized the lanyard, gave a mighty shout and pulled. A flash of flame sprang from the muzzle, a thunderous boom and a pall of gunsmoke followed : I didn't even see the duck jump.

Rising to my knees I seized the setting pole and urged the punt forward through the pall of smoke. My shot had been right on the mark, a large number of duck lay dead along the water's edge, several cripples were walking shoreward across the mud, while about a dozen were swimming rapidly off down the river. Dropping the grapnel over the stern, I filled my pocket with cartridges from the ammo' tin, pulled the cripple stopper from under the deck, and set off at top speed across the mud to deal with the " walking wounded." These I shot as quickly as possible, leaving them where they lay.

Returning to the punt I scanned the river through the glasses, counting the swimmers and noting their position. Luckily most of the cripples had remained in one group, but they were going downstream fast and had covered a considerable distance before I finally overtook them. Even then it took quite a while to deal with them, as many dived repeatedly and surfaced, showing only the top of their heads, which, in the rough water, were very difficult to spot, let alone hit ! By the time I had accounted for the last cripple I was well over a mile below the scene of the shot. At this stage I had retrieved only a handful of birds and now began the hectic business of the pickup. The drill, as always, was to get below the bird furthest downstream, and this I did, scooping it up with the landing net followed by several others that were drifting down close behind it. Because of the strength of the current it was impossible to hold my position in mid-river for long, and I was compelled to wait in the slack water near the river's edge, and as each bird drifted down I would row out across the current and net it. Since the birds were following quite close behind each other I was kept very busy for a time.

At last no more wigeon were in sight and I set out to work the punt upstream towards the scene of the shot, sometimes poling along the edge and at others " walking " the punt along where the going was firm enough. During this period I kept a sharp look-out for any other duck drifting down the river, but since the wind was now blowing freshly on to " my " side, I expected to find that most of the dead duck in the vicinity of the shot would have blown ashore. This proved to be the case, and when I eventually regained the scene I found that nearly all the duck which had fallen in the water were strewn along the shore only a short distance downstream. The remainder of the pick-up was comparatively easy, and after a careful search of the area I ended up with 61 wigeon, two of which had unfortunately been spoiled by a pair of greater black-back gulls which had turned up during my absence.

Tide Flight

Ferryman

. . . the incoming duck were almost unshootable

John Marchington

THE day had started most inauspiciously, for although Hugh and I had been out on the shore since before daybreak, and it was now almost one o'clock in the afternoon, neither of us had fired a single shot . . . or even looked liked firing one. Admittedly we had seen plenty of stuff in the course of the morning; long skeins of geese, totalling well over 2,000, that had come off the sands at first light with a strong and bitter wind in their tails, to go gabbling off inland 400 feet high or more, disappearing for the rest of the day. Great flights of curlew that came hurtling along before the wind to go into the most fantastic evasive manoeuvres when they spotted us standing behind the cut bank, not bothering to hide from them. There were black rafts of duck, miles away on the tideline, so far away indeed, that even the binoculars failed to identify them positively, although we knew that they must be wigeon. The duck seemed strangely restless, party after party rising at intervals and flying up and down the tideline in ever-widening circles as the flood tide began to move up the bay.

It was this constant movement that gave us the idea of a tide flight, so making the best speed possible back to the car, we drove round to the head of the bay and parked close to the shore in a position from which we could watch developments through the glasses. Almost at once it was apparent that we had made a good move, for small parties of duck were already flighting well in over the mud flats ; many were following the line of a large drain that meandered across the flats almost directly opposite our viewpoint.

Following the line of the big drain, or creek to use the local term, we headed out on to the flats, leaning into the strong wind which at times almost blew us to a standstill. Suddenly Hugh pointed to seaward . . . a party of about 20 wigeon were heading straight for us, travelling at a tremendous pace before the wind. We immediately jumped down into the creek and crouched below the level of the bank, but the wigeon, after coming to within about 100 yards of our position, turned into the wind, and swooping down to within a few yards of the mud, flew back towards the sea. As soon as the coast was clear we hurried forward through the soft mud, and, somewhat breathlessly, took up positions about where we estimated the wigeon had turned back. We hadn't long to wait. Almost at once another party came in on exactly the same line, but when almost within shot they also turned and headed out towards the sea. When this had happened once again we decided to move still further seaward, and as soon as the duck were out of sight, we did so, moving forward at least 150 yards and taking cover in a steep-walled creek.

Since the incoming duck were almost unshootable, owing to their height and speed, we agreed to let everything go past and take them only on their return flight, when they would be lower and slower. The first to arrive at our new position was a single wigeon which went whistling over our heads, turned back and came past me on my left. My shot was right on the mark and he dropped on to the mud a considerable distance away, having been blown backwards by the wind as he fell. Having no dog with us we left him where he fell and soon we were back in business again.

This time a scattered party of about 30 wigeon went tearing past us, and as they came out again, following the line of the creek, Hugh cut down a cock with a shot from his single-barrelled gun, and as they flared I managed to knock down a couple. A few minutes later this success was repeated, and again we had three birds down for our three shots. Shortly afterwards I had another chance at a party of about seven wigeon somewhat wide of me on my left, but made a mess of it, with the result that the only bird hit came down a long way off, and was clearly a runner. There being nothing else for it, I immediately set off to attempt to retrieve this bird, which I eventually succeeded in doing after a long hard slog. In the course of this retrieve I kept a wary eye to seaward, and each time I saw duck on the move I crouched low on the mud with the result that Hugh had several shots during this interval, most of them successful. It was, in fact, extremely interesting to watch the duck approach Hugh's hidden position, suddenly to go shooting straight up into the air with usually one dead bird falling to the mud as the almost inaudible sound of the shot reached my ears. By the time

I rejoined him in the creek Hugh had four more duck down, three wigeon and a pintail, the latter one of a pair that had given him a splendid chance for a right and left, if only he had had a left to use. This, of course, is one of the snags of using a single-barrelled gun, but Hugh shoots so well with this gun that it probably pays off in the long run.

The flight continued at intervals for the next half hour or so during which time each of us added several more wigeon to the bag. There isn't the slightest doubt that we would have added more had it not been for the fact that our feet were completely stuck in the glue-like mud of the creek bottom, making it quite impossible to move at the last moment. This meant that we had to try to estimate on which side of us the duck would pass and set ourselves facing in that direction in good time. If the duck changed direction at the last moment, which they sometimes did, it was usually very difficult and often impossible to get a shot at them at all. Nevertheless, the flight was tremendously exciting, since the duck were on the move almost continuously, and there was never a dull moment.

But all good things come to an end ! Round a' bend in the creek swept the incoming tide, quickly deepening and making it necessary for us to pack up with the utmost speed lest the creeks behind us fill up and cut us off from the merse. Even so the " pick-up " took some time since the duck were scattered about over a wide area of soft mud, but eventually we accounted for them all except Hugh's pintail. What happened to this bird we never discovered. Perhaps it recovered and flew away, although we doubt this very much. On reaching the merse edge, very hot and out of puff, despite the cold wind, we laid out the bag to admire and count; we had picked up 21 wigeon, all shot in a little over an hour and a half.

Ferryman's
Lucky BBs
Five cartridges, five geese!

JUST before my friend Graham left for his home in the south following a brief, but fairly successful joint foray against the geese, he bequeathed to me what was left of his small stock of Maximum BBs, and the luck those few cartridges brought me has been quite astonishing.

Having a free afternoon, a few days after my friend departed, I decided to visit the "Wee Merse" in the hope that even at this unlikely time of day I might be lucky enough to get a shot at some of the pinkfeet I knew were frequenting the area. On arriving at the farm where the car was to be left I climbed into my fowling gear, buckled on my cartridge belt which was already filled with a variety of cartridges and at the last moment put halfa-dozen of Graham's BBs into the pocket of my anorak. With my bitch Candy at heel I made my way down the rough and muddy track leading to the merse edge, and as I approached the high turf bank flanking the merse I slipped a couple of Graham's BBs into the chambers of the magnum.

The gun had barely clicked shut when I heard the high-pitched calling of pink-feet approaching from seaward, and without trying to spot them I covered the short remaining distance at top speed, and flung myself, panting, down behind the bank. Regaining my breath I crawled to the top of the bank and peeped over. Five pinkfeet were flying almost straight at me at no great height and were already within gunshot! Moments later, with cries of alarm, they suddenly flared and swung away to the left . . . unnoticed by me the dog had walked to the top of the bank and was standing in full view! Hastily rising to my knees I fired at the last bird of the party which collapsed at the shot. Swinging well ahead I fired at the next in line, now rapidly getting out of range, and this bird after wobbling along for a short distance also fell stone dead. Ejecting the spent cases I looked at them approvingly and popped another couple into the gun. Candy brought the two geese, which proved to be young birds and quite small.

Moving out on to the merse I found it liberally sprinkled with goose droppings and was looking around for a suitable creek in which to hide when I once again heard goose music. The only handy creek was somewhat shallow but I dived into this, wedging the dog firmly between my knees. Peering cautiously over the creek edge I could see a skein of about 30 pinkfeet approaching from the same direction as the first party, but flying considerably higher. However they were still within range of the grcund so I crouched as low as possible and kept as still as a mouse.

. . . a skein of greylags . . . Pamela Harrison

On they came, gabbling away like mad, and when they were almost overhead I stood up and fired once —twice—and two geese were plummeting to the ground.

To say I was delighted with my performance is to put it mildly—here was a really good right and left taken from a position that was far from ideal, the sort of thing that makes up for many, many disappointments. Come to think of it two rights and lefts, and both within a few minutes of arriving at the scene of the fray. Oh Graham ! if only you had been there to see what luck your "maxis" brought me! These geese were much larger than the first two which were obviously birds of the year, the original five probably being a family party. Having set up four dead geese to act as decoys I once again went to earth in the creek, but although one or two other lots of geese flew up or down the estuary none came near enough for a shot. Then, just as the light was beginning to fade and I thought my shooting was over for the day, a skein of greylags came gabbling down-river and pitched on the merse edge about half a mile from my stance. On studying the position through my binoculars it became obvious that these geese were stalkable, but this would mean a long slog through the soft mud of the river edge with the possibility that something or someone would move them before I got close enough to do any good. Nevertheless, the more I looked the more certain I became that I could get within range of this lot, especially when my luck was so obviously in. Carefully hiding the four pinkfeet and all my surplus gear except the binoculars and with Graham's two remaining BBs chambered, I set out on the stalk.

To begin with I made good progress as I was able to keep well up the bank where the mud was reasonably firm, but as I neared the geese I was forced to go lower and lower down in order to keep out of sight. Here the soft mud took its toll and I plowtered along in a lather of sweat, puffing and panting like an old grampus, with only the "goose fever" left to keep me going. Eventually I reached a position which I estimated was little more than 150 yards from the nearest geese, but before I attempted the final crawl up the mud slope, I needed a rest. Kneeling down, I leaned on the dog for support, and after a minute or so was just at the point of moving when it happened . . . two loud reports from the other side of the river . . . an evening flighter had opened up!

The geese, which had been buzzing away happily all this time, instantly went quiet; for a long minute or so, while I hastily scrabbled up the mud slope on "three legs," nothing happened, and I was just beginning to hope that miraculously they were going to stay put when, with a roar of wings, they were up and away. Lying face downwards on the mud I watched out of the tail of my eye, the geese swing round to my right, pivoting on the birds nearest to me. As they passed behind me I rolled over on to my back, sat up and fired one somewhat forlorn shot at the end bird of the line ; to my joy he went into a dive which ended when he hit the mud with a terrific splosh. The dog plunged out through the soft mud and with considerable difficulty brought the goose to hand. It proved to be a very large bird, even for a grey-lag, and was surprisingly heavy. At one stage Candy had found it almost impossible to lift it clear of the mud into which her feet were sinking deeply, and I had a few anxious moments while she struggled gamely through this soft patch.

With a certain amount of trepidation I later presented this bird to some relatives, explaining that because of its size I feared it might be somewhat tough, which might well have been the understatement of the year! I was all the more pleased therefore to be later informed that it was the finest and tastiest goose they had ever eaten !

Wigeon Under the Moon

Ferryman enjoys a class flight

Pamela Harrison

ALTHOUGH I rarely go moonlighting flighting nowadays there was a time when every suitable moonlight night found me out on the merse, sometimes with one or more companions, often alone. The main quarry was the greylag goose, for although nowadays we have sometimes large numbers of pinkfeet in our estuary, the "greys" were the only type of geese usually found there in those days. A close second came the wigeon, and there can be hardly anything more exciting than a big wigeon flight under the moon, particularly when the sky has just the right amount of cloud to silhouette the duck clearly. This, in fact, is absolutely essential as it is almost impossible to see the duck against a clear sky.

My most successful wigeon flight occurred one Saturday evening when all signs indicated that it was more likely to end in complete failure, and that evening as I rowed across the estuary in the old black punt so aptly named "The Coffin," I was in a far from optimistic mood. There was little enough to be optimistic about; the evening was completely windless, the water glassy calm, and the punt ploughed a straight furrow down the sunpath as the fiery red orb sank towards the horizon. As I rowed, I scanned the sky for any Sign of cloud, but apart from a long bank low on the western horizon, into which the sun was about to set, there wasn't a vestige of cloud to be seen. Anchoring the punt I made my way right out towards the merse edge where I thought there was just the possibility that I might get a chance at some geese as they flighted out at the darkening to roost on the high sands. Already the curlew were fighting, their orderly lines interspersed by the more ragged formations of gulls which were coming off the land in large numbers to join the many hundreds already at roost on the sands.

By the time I reached my chosen stance the sun had disappeared behind the cloudbank and in that direction the sky was a blaze of reddish light against which the fighting gulls looked jet black. Gradually the light faded and in the deepening twilight I several times heard geese talking, and once glimpsed their distant line as they flew out over the sands to whiffle down to their roosts. It had been my intention to take the evening flight and then, if conditions were suitable, to await moonrise, which would be about an hour after dark. I had calculated that the wigeon might well wait until flood-tide and then flight under the moon. The first part of my calculations appeared to be correct at any rate, for by the time it was too dark to see properly I had neither seen nor heard a wigeon.

Having decided that unless some cloud had appeared by moonrise I would call it a day, I made my way back to where the punt lay at anchor. By the time I got there the sky was lightening along the crest of the hills to the east, and soon the moon, like a great cheese, swam into view, bathing the merse in dim orange light. At almost the same time I heard the purl of the flooding tide and felt a breath of cold wind on my face. Looking up I could see streaks of wispy cloud drifting across the face of the moon. All was not yet lost!

Some time later, lying face upwards in the bottom of the punt to keep out the fresh and bitterly cold breeze that was blowing, I smoked a cigarette and watched a transformation take place in the sky above. In a remarkably short time almost the entire sky was covered with a layer of thin cloud, softly lit from behind by the moon ... a perfect " shooter's sky." Once again I walked out on to the merse, and had gone only a very short distance when I heard the whistling of approaching wigeon. Dropping on one knee I looked in the direction of the sound, and suddenly there they were, a little party of wigeon, clearly silhouetted against the sky and circling the merse not very far in front of me with the apparent intention of landing. Sure enough ... down they went, invisible against the dark grass, and immediately I hurried in their direction, putting them up almost at once. Looking around the area in which they had pitched I found a little creek in which to hide, and had barely taken cover when once again the whistling of the cocks announced the arrival of more wigeon. These birds flew around for a short time and then pitched almost within range. I had still not fired a shot, but my chance wasn't long in coming. A chorus of whee-ohs, and a party of wigeon swung across my front, forming a sort of ball as they did so. Two quick shots into the brown and the whole expedition was suddenly worthwhile as three wigeon dropped to the ground.

From then on the fun was fast and furious, there being few intervals during which it wasn't possible to see or hear wigeon flying around or even pitching within sight or sound. Having no dog I was obliged to pick up each bird as soon as it was dawn, and only this fact prevented me from running out of cartridges long before the flight was over. However, it was absolutely essential to do this, otherwise I would have lost many birds. Even as it was, several of them took a lot of finding, and I lost many chances while searching for dead or wounded birds. In the end it did not matter very much, for as the flight petered out I was reduced to firing my "goose cartridges," having nothing else left. This was by far the best and most exciting moonlight wigeon flight of my lifetime, and even though my shooting left a lot to be desired, when I counted the heap of duck lying by my stance in the creek, they added up to a very satisfactory 27 wigeon.

As I rowed homewards across the now very choppy water of the estuary I wondered how long it would be before I bettered that score. I haven't done so yet!

Hugh's Goose

Ferryman sees a chance taken

. . . the geese came off the sands heavens high . . .   Pamela Harrison

MY young friend Hugh is, without doubt, one of the keenest wildfowlers I have ever known, and, despite the vast discrepancy in our years, it is a pleasure to go out with him. To Hugh no hour is too ungodly to get out of bed, no weather too cold, wet or miserable in which to set out, no creek too muddy in which to hide, and no day too long. Unfortunately, in order to earn a livelihood, Hugh, like so many others, is compelled to do his shooting as and when opportunity offers. Holidays apart, his only free day being Saturday, he has been compelled, in local parlance, to join the " Saturday Army." This immediately places him at a serious disadvantage, and one from which I used to suffer myself, for the plain truth is, that on most Saturdays more gunners are abroad on the foreshore of this district than there is room for. Despite all this, Hugh, who is something of a goose addict, enjoys a reasonable degree of success, and usually manages to include a number of these birds in his bag . . . but not this season . .. or at any rate this was the position when we set out on the morning of the final Saturday.

Now this, to my friend, was a lamentable state of affairs, almost incredible in fact. Hadn't he always managed to bag at least one goose ? Even in his very first season, when armed only with a single .410 ? Admittedly he had stalked that one and shot it sitting, but even so . . . true he had actually shot a goose this season when out alone, but by the greatest misfortune this bird had fallen in the sea much too far out for his little spaniel to retrieve safely, so Hugh had very wisely refrained from sending her after it. Now here we were, with Hugh still gooseless, on his very last outing of the season.

Despite our prayers for a gale of wind or at the very least half a gale, the day opened calm and still with a sharp frost that coated everything in a thick layer of white rime. As was to be expected in the circumstances, the geese came off the sands heavens high, and although we knew from the number of parked cars, that the estuary was well ringed by gunners, not a shot was fired as the cackling skeins winged their way inland. Now this fact alone emphasised the height at which the geese had flighted, for we knew only too well that had they been down, even to about the 300ft mark, some gunner who fancied he was armed with a super weapon, would have had a go !

Having decided to make a day of it whatever the weather, we moved out on to the mud flats as soon as the tide permitted and took cover under the edge of a large creek. Here we hoped to get a few shots at duck with just *perhaps* a chance at an odd goose, although this, we thought, was a pretty forlorn hope. We had barely settled in however, When we spotted a small party of greylags at shootable height, flying in from seaward. These geese, which at one time looked as though they might give us a chance, eventually passed about a couple of hundred yards wide of us on our left. Our first reaction was to move over to this line and we very nearly did so, but after some discussion we decided not to. Shortly afterwards we had reason to regret this decision as four more greylags, also at shootable height, came in on almost exactly the same line as the first lot.

Although I had an uneasy feeling that we were probably doing the wrong thing. I now proposed that we should move, with which proposal my young friend heartily agreed. Ah! woe is me ! Not another goose came within miles of us, but about half-an-hour later seven mallard, soon followed by three others, actually pitched within a few yards of our previous hide-out. After a somewhat abortive attempt to stalk these duck we decided to split forces, Hugh returning to stand No. 1, while I remained at stand No. 2, and in these positions we remained until the returning tide forced us to retreat.

During all this time we managed to bag only two duck, Hugh getting a single teal, the only chance that came his way, and I a wigeon which I knocked out of a small party from which I ought to have had a couple. Returning to the car, we motored round the estuary to another part of the shore where we proposed to await the evening flight, and on arrival found no less than five cars already parked at the merse edge . . . we were evidently going to have plenty of company ! After a longish walk we eventually found a space sufficiently far removed from our nearest neighbours to be safe from any lead that might be flying about in the gloaming. Here we took cover among some tide-worn tussocks right out on the merse edge, and in the gathering dusk settled down to await the flight.

It was still completely windless and the gull and wader hordes were making their usual evening clamour as they assembled in their thousands at no great distance from our hideout. Suddenly, above the cacophany of sound, we heard a pinkfoot calling, and soon we spotted a single goose flying above the sands and parallel with the merse. As it passed us and disappeared into the gloom Hugh turned to me with a rueful smile, " Hang it," said he, " there goes my last chance for this season, it looks as though I'm not going to get a goose after all."

" Well, I'm afraid you're right, son," I replied, " unless of course a miracle occurs." We both laughed, not believing much in miracles.

Now, what happened afterwards is hard to believe, but only a minute or two after these words were spoken, a shot rang out from the direction of our nearest neighbours . . . two gunners who were concealed in a hide about 200 yards from our position, and somewhat inshore of us. Turning quickly we could see that the shot had evidently been fired at a single pinkfoot, probably the same goose that we had seen go past in the opposite direction a few minutes earlier. It was now heading in our general direction, but was gradually angling off. Hastily, Hugh ejected the cartridge from his single 12-bore and reloaded with a Hymax Treble A. " Shall I try it ? " he whispered urgently, " it's a long shot."

" You bet," I replied, " but mind you give it plenty of lead."

Hugh straightened up, swung well ahead and fired. The goose staggered at the shot, its legs dropped down, but it carried on, its head weaving from side to side. Suddenly it lost balance and crashed among the stranded ice floes 100 yards out on the sands. Hugh gave a Whoop of triumph. " You said it needed a miracle, well what about that then ? "

Loading a muzzle-loader

The Punt

by Ferryman

FOR many years I had longed to own a punt and puntgun of my own; not that I had been entirely deprived of participation in this wonderful form of sport for lack of one . . . far from it ! Since my first memorable foray with the Major at the age- of 13, I had from time to time the great good fortune to be invited to accompany him and other puntsmen on expeditions in our own and neighbouring estuaries. Among these gentlemen were one or two of the best and most experienced puntsmen of their day. Better still, my good friend Adam, of whom I have written before, and to whom I remain eternally grateful, when not punting himself, was usually very willing to lend me either his single or double punt with his little " half-pound " breech-loading gun. This generosity opened the door to exciting opportunities, and although workaday ties greatly restricted the number of outings, I alone in the single, or accompanied by my brother Jack or a friend in the double punt, was able to enjoy the matchless thrill of seeking the wildfowl on their own ground . . . . the great sandbanks and mudflats of the estuary, the last of the wild and lonely places left to us.

In those far-off days every opportunity was taken to get afloat, but because work had to come first, many of our outings were perforce taken at the wrong time of day and in whatever weather came our way. Inevitably this sometimes resulted in disappointment, but on the whole we fared remarkably well, and in any case the tremendous thrill and excitement was never absent from these outings. Long before there was the slightest hope of my doing so I made up my mind that sooner or later I would acquire a punt and punt-gun of my own.

At last came the opportunity for which I had waited so long ; an advertisement in the local paper stated, " For sale, double punt and M.L. puntgun," with an address in a town on the other side of the estuary. That same evening I set out on my bike and peddled the 14 miles to the town, located the advertiser and inspected the outfit. To begin with I wasn't very impressed with what I saw. The gun, which was in a shed behind the owner's house, was a massive affair with a bore of 1¾ inches. Being a muzzle-loader it was difficult to inspect the bore, but what could be seen of the inside was somewhat rusty, and showed obvious signs of neglect. The owner appeared hurt when I pointed this out to him and assured me that the gun received regular attention. " Is it the wee pickle roost that's botherin' ye son ? " he enquired, " you needna' worry aboot that, it's only floatin' ! Besides," he enthused, " it's a grand killer, there's no' a better ane in the whole o' Scotland ! . .." " And look at a' that stuff," he added, indicating a pile of gear among which I noted a large ammunition box filled with all sorts of treasures, a ramrod, copper charger, several tins of gunpowder, bags of shot, etc., etc. "There's mair than three stane o' B.B. shot among that lot, an' I'll no' tak' an extra ha'penny for it." I looked around at the gear as a miser must look at his hoard, felt myself being carried away, and in order to bring myself back to earth I seized hold of the great gun . . . it was all I could do to lift it off the floor !

The punt was lying on the grass down by the harbour, and thither we went to inspect it. At first glance it appeared to be all right, but I got a shock when I looked into the cockpit and found the grass growing up through her bottom seams! " Ooh that's all right," her owner assured me, "a wee while in the water and she'll tak' up and no' leak a cupfa'." I wasn't so sure. After a great deal of further discussion and bargaining a provisional price was agreed. It was arranged that I would think the matter over and, if I decided to buy, I would telephone the following day (Sunday) and come to collect the outfit on Monday evening. The seller agreed to have the gun and all the gear down at the harbour and would help me launch the punt ready for her voyage down the little tidal river on which the town stood, and across the estuary.

I hardly slept a wink that night, and long before morning I had made up my mind to buy the outfit despite its obvious shortcomings. Bright and early in the morning I telephoned to clinch the bargain, and the next evening, accompanied by my young nephew Alan, travelled round by bus to collect my new possessions. The seller, as arranged, had everything ready, and since we had a long way to go, the punt was quickly dragged to the edge of the mud and slid down into the water where it immediately started to fill ! With all possible speed the gun and the rest of the gear were put aboard, and with young Alan bailing steadily, we pushed off and swept down river in the strong current. As he waved us goodbye, I had an uneasy feeling that the seller looked distinctly worried ! The punt dropped rapidly downstream towards the main river channel which I was anxious to reach before the flood tide set in. Unfortunately, despite Allan's bailing, it soon became obvious that the water was gaining on him, so I was several times forced to run the punt ashore and assist him in bailing it dry. These delays cost us dear, for while we were still some distance from the main channel, we were caught by the flood tide which came roaring upstream with such force, that it was impossible to hold our position in mid-river, let alone make any headway against it. Nothing else for it then but to row ashore and " walk " the punt against the tide in the shallow water along the river's edge. This was slow and gruelling work, as with each step we sank into the soft mud almost to the knees. This laborious stage in our voyage was, fortunately, relieved by the sight of large numbers of wigeon, newly arrived in the estuary, which came sweeping up in rafts on the flood tide, some allowing themselves to be carried quite close to us before taking wing. Even under the stresses of the moment they were a heartening sight.

Eventually we reached the junction of the main channel, now over a mile wide, or rather it reached us, as the tide swept rapidly over the mudflats. The tide, however, was now in our favour, so waiting only long enough to once again bail out the punt, we set out on this, the only really risky part of our voyage, hoping that by now the seams would be " taking up " somewhat. Alas for hope ; if anything the punt appeared to be leaking worse than ever, and I was compelled to stop rowing from time to time in order to help Alan get the water level down, as I knew only too well the danger of allowing even a few inches of water to accumulate in a punt with a heavy gun on deck. Even so, when we finally made the " hard " on our own side of the estuary, an acquaintance who had been watching our approach in the gathering dusk, said we had appeared to be sitting rowing " on a plank," so low in the water had the punt sunk.

Less than a fortnight later that same punt, painted, caulked and as tight as a bottle, was in action against the wigeon. The big gun, nick-named " Gus " after its former owner, boomed out its first broadside, and proved that it was indeed a " grand killer," yes ! quite probably the best of its kind in Scotland !

Morning on the Island

Ferryman

Small parties of greylags used the island as a roost.　　　J. A. Schrijnder

OFF the wide sandy estuary of a river a dozen or so miles from my home, lies a group of small rocky islands. Certain of these can be reached on foot at low water on any ordinary tide, but the outermost pair, which are separated from each other by a narrow sound, can only be reached on foot during the period of spring tides, as only then does the tide ebb far enough out.

During spring and summer these islands are noisy with a milling mass of seafowl, as hundreds of pairs of herring gulls nest here, together with smaller numbers of greater and lesser blackbacks and the not so common common gull. Round the island's perimeter are a sprinkling of oyster-catchers, while under overturned rocks a few pairs of shelduck breed. In the hollows among the tussocks of long coarse grass, with which much of the island is covered, can still be found an occasional down-covered clutch of mallard eggs. For many years considerable numbers of these duck nested here, but when rats appeared on the islands the number of nesting mallard dwindled rapidly. How the gulls survive the depredations of the rats is anybody's guess; probably they suffer heavy losses of eggs and young and only their numbers ensure a degree of successful breeding which they undoubtedly achieve. Although mallard no longer breed here in any numbers, they still use the islands as a winter haunt, as do certain other duck including a fair number of teal and wigeon.

The ideal morning is one with a strong off-shore wind, for not only does this usually result in a longer ebb, but it discourages the duck from pitching in the sea, which they are prone to do in calm weather. On windy mornings the duck usually come right in with the intention of landing on the seaweed-covered rocks and can usually be dropped well clear of the water which even at low tide surrounds nine-tenths of the islands. None the less, one of the most eventful and satisfactory shoots I ever enjoyed here was on a morning of almost glassy calm. By good luck my day "off duty" happened to fall on a morning when low tide coincided with first light and I decided to try my luck on the islands. I was naturally disappointed to find it an almost windless morning, but having made up my mind to go I got out the old motor-bike, and with gun and gamebag slung over my shoulders, *phut-phutted* off to the shore.

On arrival I parked the bike by the beach and set out across the mile or so of firm sand towards the inshore tip of the larger island, the only point that would ebb dry. As I neared the island the sky was already lightening and as I waded the final stretch through the still ebbing tide I could hear mallard quacking somewhere ahead of me. Once safely on the island I loaded my gun and made my way round the rocky shore towards the " Sound " where I intended to take up my flighting stance. The light was rapidly improving and I hurried along at my best speed over the rough going. Several times I both heard and saw duck, once or twice within reasonable range, but always they were out over the water, and would have been difficult to retrieve had I succeeded in dropping any, so I held my fire. Suddenly I heard the low-pitched gaga of approaching geese, and out of the gloom to my left front there appeared a little skein of greylag flying parallel to the shore and less than 30ft above the sea.

Crouching among the rocks I waited with pounding heart until the geese were almost directly opposite me, swung ahead of the leader and fired. The charge of No 5 shot caught him fair and square, and down he went into the sea with a great splash ; as the surviving geese lifted I fired at the nearest and it followed the leader into the sea. Scrambling down to the water's edge I made sure that both geese were dead, and then set about the task of retrieving them. I already knew that the water at this point was much too deep to wade ; the geese were only about 20 yards out from the rocks, but the still ebbing tide was already at work and the gap was steadily widening. If the geese were to be retrieved there was only one way to do it ! Hastily discarding my heavy winter clothing I tiptoed gingerly over the freezing cold seaweed to the water's edge. Shivering for a moment on the brink, I took another look at the drifting geese to give me courage, leaned well forward and plunged in head first ! I will never forget the icy cold of that water ! Surfacing, I struck out at top speed for the nearest goose, grabbed it by the neck and headed for the second. After an unsuccessful attempt to hold both geese in one hand, I seized the wing-tip of the second in my teeth and nudging it ahead of me with my head, made for the shore. Drying myself as best I could I scrambled back into my clothing and leaving the geese among the rocks to be picked up on my return journey, I hurried along to the Sound. Despite the bitter cold of the water I had been in and out so quickly that in the few minutes it took to reach my destination, I was as warm as ever. Almost at once I heard the *yeebing* of a mallard drake, and, turning, spotted him heading through the Sound from the seaward end. A quick shot and down he went into water only about knee deep and was easily retrieved. Shortly afterwards three mallard, two ducks and a drake, came through from the opposite end. A shot at the leader brought both it and the following duck down dead, and a second shot accounted for the drake. This astonishing piece of luck, following the successful shots at the geese, set the seal on the morning's sport, and although most of the remaining duck I saw landed on the sea well out of range, the day was already made.

Just before I packed up, a nice bunch of teal whizzed by from behind me, and having taken me completely by surprise, were almost out of range before I got the gun up. The one shot I got off failed to connect and immediately afterwards I decided to make my way to the other end of the island, as I estimated that the flood tide was about due. Having picked up the two geese *en route* I had almost reached the " dry " end of the island when I spotted a single mallard approaching low over the water. This bird pitched on the sea close inshore and almost immediately swam right in to the beach. Using some intervening rocks as cover, I stalked as close to the spot as possible and peeped cautiously over the top expecting to find the duck sitting in plain view. Not a sign ! I had just made up my mind that it must have flown off unseen when it suddenly clattered up from amongst some seaweed-covered boulders right under my nose. In my haste to drop it before it got too far out over the water I fired too soon and clean missed it with my first shot. A second shot, however, taken with less haste, brought it down with a splash in what I discovered was only thigh-deep water from which it was retrieved without difficulty.

I had judged the tide very well and by the time I was ready to quit the island it was already flowing, creeping across the sands in a relentless flood. However, laden as I was with my spoils, I was easily able to keep ahead of it and reached the mainland safely and very happy.

Opening Shoot

Ferryman has good sport in early September

Pamela Harrison

OPENING day this season for my young friend Hugh and I occurred on Saturday, September 5, not, I hasten to add, by choice, but simply by force of circumstances. For weeks prior to this we had reconnoitred all the likely places, and finally decided that our eagerly anticipated opening shoot would take place at a somewhat distant venue. Here, a small burn debouched on to the sandflats and reconnaissance had shown that it was regularly being used by mallard which were apparently feeding in adjacent barley stubbles. The place certainly didn't look very promising, since the part of the burn frequented by the duck meandered through an area almost as flat as a board. Indeed the only vestige of cover was the tip of a stony beach which at one point stuck out to within a gunshot of the burn. At first sight it looked a pretty hopeless proposition, but past experience had shown that it was possible to construct a hide on this spot, building up the limited quantity of loose stones available in the form of a low butt and topping this with twigs draped with seaweed, of which there was a plentiful supply.

Five o'clock found us already hard at work on the hide ; we were in high spirits for weather conditions could hardly have been better. A strong offshore wind was blowing exactly as we had prayed it would. The sky was cloudy, but not too cloudy, letting through sufficient dawn-light to enable us to see what we were doing. By the time it was possible to distinguish objects clearly enough to shoot, the hide was finished, and we were snugly hidden, Hugh facing to landward and I watching the seaward approaches.

Apart from the arrival of sundry curlew and other waders, including a solitary greenshank, nothing of moment occurred for a longish time. We were pleased enough to see the waders, for many of them passed within close range of the hide and not a few, including the greenshank, actually pitched in or near the burn right "under our guns." The fact that they took absolutely no notice was very heartening, as we had built up the hide somewhat higher than usual and feared that it might be too conspicuous. The first excitement arose when two duck-like forms, followed at a short distance by a third, were observed approaching from seaward.

"Shellers" (shelduck) hissed Hugh, as the leading pair crossed our line of fire. Gun muzzles were lowered, we relaxed, a moment later the third bird, quacking loudly, slowed off into the gloom . . . a mallard duck. A sheepish look at each other, "Oh well, not to worry; there'll be plenty more where that one came from." A few minutes later a little party of duck approached from the same direction. Their silhouettes appeared rather small for mallard, but Hugh shook his " quacker " vigorously at them just the same. As they swung round the front of the hide, we both fired, each of us getting one bird down. Candy, my labrador, rushed out to retrieve, and we were not altogether surprised when she returned with the very first wigeon of the season. She had just returned with the second when a pair of mallard, quickly joined by several others, appeared out of the gloom to landward and pitched alongside the burn just out of effective range. We were debating whether or not to move this lot, which we felt might decoy others away from us, when the matter was settled by the arrival of a single mallard drake which fell to my second shot as he swooped down to join the previous arrivals.

From then on there was seldom a dull moment, with duck appearing at intervals from all angles and presenting us with some very difficult shots. The excitement was tremendous and although our shooting was anything but good the bag continued to grow steadily. By an unlucky chance we were twice caught with empty guns by large flights of mallard . . . by far the best chances of the morning . . . which swept past unsaluted, at point blank range. None the less, our indifferent shooting was highlighted by a number of really good efforts, the kind of shots that "make the day". Such as the mallard drake coming down-wind at a terrific speed and which, taken well in front by Hugh, whistled stone dead right over our heads and crashed a long way out on the sands; or the single very high pintail which fell to my shot when, because of the tremendous lead I had given it, I feared I might have missed in front.

The presence of the pintail, and indeed of the wigeon had come as a pleasant surprise to us, since we had expected to see only mallard and perhaps a few teal. In the event a fair number of pintail turned up, rather fewer wigeon, but not a single teal. The grand finale occurred in broad daylight just after we had decided that the flight was over for the morning; a pair of mallard coming in on my side of the butt were taken well in front. At the instant the gun muzzle was raised to blot out the leading bird, the two birds appeared almost as one and when they reappeared over the gun barrels they were both "dead in the air."

The opening shoot had been an unqualified success and even Candy looked pleased as she posed beside the bag. Ten handsome mallard, their crops bulging with barley, lay there. Three pintail, and three wigeon made up the rest.

Someone once said that God gave us our memory
so that we could gather roses in December.

For those readers who like me are approaching 'December',
I hope that the stories have rekindled many happy memories,
and for the younger practitioners in the sport of
wildfowling that they will find much to interest them,
and to have learnt more about the wonderful area of the
Solway Firth.

Desmond Batley

Appendix

Howard Hughes enjoying a tea break

Creetown Annie

The History of the *Creetown Annie*
by John Scoular

The vessel was reputedly built at Arnside, a famous yard for fishing boats in the north of England. This ties in with some local history since there was a migration of fishing families, often with their vessels to the Scottish side of the Solway some time in the 1800s.

Certainly the *Annie* was around well before the First World War and probably before the end of the previous century since she is listed in some of the very early regatta programmes, a few of which can be seen in the Steam Packet Hotel in the Isle of Whithorn. Most of my information came from the late Charlie McGuire, a contemporary fisherman with Adam Birrell. In fact the pair of them were very much sought after speakers or lecturers in their latter years, scorning to appear in other than their traditional fishermans' jerseys and 'fearnought' trousers.

The *Annie* was a half ton mussel boat, her principal work involving dropping down Wigtown Bay on the ebb tide, grounding on the mussel bank, loading up and back up to Creetown on the flood where the mussels were cleaned, barreled and off to market at the railway station. She was also used for all manner of other fishing and wildfowling duties. The *Annie* measured approximately twenty feet overall and was owned by the famous fisherman Adam Birrell for most of her life. She was reputed to have boasted three different sets of sails: winter working, summer working and a special set for racing. She was well known and highly successful at the important local regattas where the prize money was very substantial for the era.

Entered for both rowing and sailing events as she could be beached in between and a special iron keel fitted for the sailing races, the *Annie* was also involved in some of the many rescue operations that Adam took part in and carried many famous people including the naturalist Peter Scott and the actor James Robertson Justice.

Mr McGuire told me that while Adam owned the boat his brother owned the mast, spar and sails—but I do not know the truth of this.

Hugh with Willie's dog Candy at Glenluce in the 1970s

Hugh Grey of Creetown went to school with Howard Hughes, Willie's son. He was taught shooting by Willie and was given the use of a Reilly shore gun by a local farmer. Having taken what his family could use he would, after a days shooting sell the surplus to local people. He would get ten shillings for a brace of mallard, half a crown for a teal, pintail or widgeon and one pound for a pheasant. He also netted for eels and eventually became an independent pest controller for local farmers.

Up until the late 1960s there was a demand for fox pelts from a firm in Argyll and he would receive eighteen to twenty pounds for one in good condition. Hugh also shot a lot with Robert McGuffie from Creetown who only had one arm. Hugh recalls Robert punting by himself which must have been very difficult when you consider his disability, and he also went punting with James Robertson Justice.

TELEGRAMS:
"FREELAND, FISHMARKET, GLASGOW."
TELEPHONE: BELL 0780

OFFICE: GALLERY, FISHMARKET

FISHMARKET
GLASGOW _16 12   19_
C.1

Sold on Account of _Wm. Hughes_
9 St. John Street Creetown

By ALEX. FREELAND & SON
WHOLESALE SALMON MERCHANTS, FISH, GAME, RABBIT & POULTRY SALESMEN

1 Bag

1 Shovellers	@ 3/3	3
2 Mallard	@ 5/6	11
2 Wigeon	@ 1/6	3
1 Grey Lag		10

£

Telegrams 1 17
Carriage ....
Market Dues 1 10   2 0
Commission ....

Nett Proceeds £   1 14 2

REMITTANCES DAILY, WEEKLY OR AS REQUESTED

PERISHABLE.   VERY URGENT.
ALEX. FREELAND & SON,
FISH, GAME, RABBIT & POULTRY SALESMEN,
CODE   FISHMARKET,
GLASGOW, C.1.

PERISHABLE.
ALEX. FREELAND & SON,
FISH, GAME, RABBIT & POULTRY SALESMEN,   VERY URGENT.
CODE
FISHMARKET,
GLASGOW, C.1.

Dear Sir,
     We herewith enclose Sales for Goods sold on your behalf,
hoping the same will be to your satisfaction.
     The continuation of your favours solicited.
       Yours truly,
         ALEX. FREELAND & SON

Sample invoice to Willie Hughes for birds, dated 1947

Bookham 54435

Our Ref: JEM/SH

W. Hughes Esq.,
5 Louden Place,
Greetown,
Newton-Stewart,
<u>WIGTOWNSHIRE.</u>

20th June, 1978.

Dear Mr. Hughes,

I really am immensely grateful to you for going to the trouble to write your very long letter of the 12th June, 1978.

I had arrived at the same conclusion as you over the origin of punt gunning, but had not localised it to the Fens. Yours is a most excellent theory, I will follow it up.

I am also very grateful for your lengthy accounts of professional punt gunners in your area. It confirms what I am discovering generally - namely, that there were no real professional punt gunners in the sense of men that did nothing else - merely countrymen, mainly fishermen who went wildfowling when the conditions were right. I will digest your letter at length when I start the punt gunning chapter in a few weeks time and I trust that you will have no objection to me paying credit to you in the book for your help.

With best wishes,

Yours sincerely,

JOHN MARCHINGTON.

Letter to Willie Hughes from John Marchington

...breaking the ice on the Cree Estuary

Adam Birrell

WAGBI
and the
SHOOTING
MAN. . . .

THE WILDFOWLERS' ASSOCIATION
of Great Britain and Ireland

Founded in 1908 by Stanley Duncan

Representing Wildfowlers and Roughshooters

President :
Rt. Hon. The Earl of Mansfield, B.A., F.Z.S., F.Z.S. (Scot.) M.B.O.U., J.P.

Chairman :
J. P. M. Wardell

Director :
John Anderton

Day's end.

Editor's Acknowledgements

My grateful thanks are due to the following:

The Shooting Times and Country Magazine, for permission to use the 'Ferryman' stories.

Howard Hughes for the use of his father's papers and for his introduction.

Andrew Macdonald who gave me the idea.

Jim Petrie and the committee of Creetown Wildfowlers.

Hugh Grey for his background knowledge.

Margaret Carrons (nee Birrell) for information on her father Adam.

John Scoular for the story of the *Creetown Annie.*

Mark Coyle for the preparation work and initial typing of the introduction.

A visit to Margaret Carrons in Dumfries resulted in additional information on her late father Adam coming to light. During our meeting she was pleased to learn that her father's boat, the *Creetown Annie* was still in good shape and is currently owned by John Scoular, a well known local sportsman and hotel owner in the Isle of Whithorn. All of these people have given freely of their time and their own contributions appear in the text at the appropriate place. Without their help, this book would not have been possible.

Desmond Batley, Editor
Wigtownshire, 2008

Further Reading

Brian Blake, *The Solway Firth,* 1966
John Marchington, *The History of Wildfowling,* 1980
Wally Wright, *Wildfowlers and Fishermen on the Solway,* 2000
The New Wildfowler, 1963

1840   **1952**

T. BLAND & SONS (Gunmakers) LTD.

NEW GUNS

Hammerless 12 Bores from £57 . 10 . 0 to £225 . 10 . 0.

3″ 12 Bore Brent Guns, £63 . 0 . 0, inc. Tax.
  (Send for Illustrated Folder.)

New Single Barrel 12 Bore Guns, B.S.A., £18 . 2 . 11. Webley, £17 . 18 . 4.
New Single barrel, Bolt action Webley 410 Guns. £9 . 7 . 6.

PUNT GUNS

Blands New 1½″ Screw Breech Gun, £125 . 0 . 0.

GUN REPAIRS

To all makes of Guns, New Barrels, Restocking, Overhauls, Recolouring, etc. Estimates
  Free. Prices Strictly Moderate.

CARTRIDGES

4, 8, 10, 12, 16, 20, 28 & 410 Bores : Alphamax, Maximum, Grand Prix, Bland Felt-
  wad, etc. (Price List on Application.)

RIFLES

22 B.S.A. Sportsman " 5," £8 . 5 . 0 ; " 15," £9 . 10 . 0 ; Brno, Winchester and
  Beretta Rifles, etc.

ACCESSORIES

Mallard Duck Decoys ...	£2 . 2 . 0 pair	**EVERYTHING FOR THE SHOOTER**
Wigeon Decoys... ...	£2 . 9 . 0 pair	Game Carriers and Bags, Cartridge Bags and Belts, Gun Cases and Covers, Cleaning Rods, etc. (Let us know your requirements and we will do our best to supply.)
Teal Decoys	£2 . 9 . 0 pair	
Wooden Feeding Pigeons	£1 . 2 . 6 each	
Improved Pigeon Decoys	4 . 6 each	Sole Agents for " English Guns and Rifles," by J. N. George, 37/6. (Trade enquiries invited.)
Silent Dog Whistles ...	15 . 4 each	

4 & 8 WILLIAM IV STREET, WEST STRAND, W.C.2

(TEMple Bar 9122)

INQUEST ON PARTRIDGES

by J. Wentworth Day

The
SHOOTING TIMES
and Country Magazine

SEVENTIETH YEAR   SATURDAY, NOVEMBER 15th, 1952   1ˢ/3ᵈ WEEKLY

THE DAWN SHOT